LIFE ON YOUR TERMS

LIFE ON YOUR TERMS

Why Doctors Use Real Estate Investments
to Set Themselves Free and How You Can Too

LETIZIA ALTO, M.D.
KENJI ASAKURA, M.D.

TAIKUN

LIFE ON YOUR TERMS

Why Doctors Use Real Estate Investments to Set Themselves Free and How You Can Too

FIRST EDITION

ISBN 978-1-5445-3096-3 *Hardcover*
      978-1-5445-3095-6 *Paperback*
      978-1-5445-3097-0 *Ebook*

For all doctors serving their patients.

*And for those who dare to dream and take
action to make their dreams a reality.*

CONTENTS

DISCLAIMER

Semi-Retired MD, Taikun LLC, and its owners, presenters, and employees are not in the business of providing personal, financial, tax, legal, or investment advice and specifically disclaim any liability, loss, or risk which is incurred as a consequence, either directly or indirectly, by the use of any of the information contained in this book. Semi-Retired MD and Taikun LLC, their websites, this book, and any online tools, if any, do NOT provide ANY legal, accounting, securities, investment, tax, or other professional services advice and are not intended to be a substitute for meeting with professional advisors. If legal advice or other expert assistance is required, the services of competent, licensed, and certified professionals should be sought. In addition, Semi-Retired MD and Taikun LLC do not endorse ANY specific investments, investment strategies, advisors, or financial service firms.

INTRODUCTION

"You'll need to find a new primary care physician," Doctor Smith said during Kenji's annual physical. "I'm making a change and will no longer be working at this clinic."

As a hospitalist himself, Kenji recognized his doctor's telltale demeanor. He looked exhausted. He didn't smile like he used to. He hadn't met him with his usual upbeat greeting upon entering the exam room. His energy was drained. Kenji saw it in his eyes, his face, and his body language.

"Are you burned out?" Kenji asked.

"Oh are you kidding me? Yes," Doctor Smith admitted, shaking his head sadly. He loved medicine and caring for patients, but he was drowning under the heavy patient load, the lack of autonomy, and the constantly shifting clinic responsibilities and metrics goals. He was transitioning to a different clinic, hoping that a new set of administrators would improve the situation and renew his passion for the profession he had once loved.

But was trading clinics really the solution? Was that going to be enough?

When we hear this story, most of us in medicine already know the answer to these questions. Switching to a different clinic or moving to a different hospital may help for a while. There are some workplaces left where doctors are not burned out, due to better administration, more freedom, and longer patient appointments. Sometimes a new environment makes all the difference in the short term.

But what about the long term? Can most of us see doing the same thing we're doing now, at the same pace, day in and day out, for the next thirty years? Our guess is most of us do not. Something has to give to make our jobs sustainable for the long term.

The truth is that this is a dark period for the American medical system. Considering how corporate medicine currently operates, it doesn't look like it's going to get better anytime soon either. In fact, it's likely that doctors will continue to shoulder an even greater burden with each passing year, like we have over the last several decades.

As doctors ourselves, Kenji and I have felt this pain.

Being a doctor today is nothing compared to being a doctor twenty or thirty years ago. The amount of data we look at for a single patient visit has ballooned significantly. As hospitalists, we review previous visits, care for patients, update families, meet with the care managers and social workers to create discharge plans, discuss the daily plan with nurses, call consults, and order labs and studies. We spend hours each day working on the electronic medical record (EMR). During the day, we are pulled in twenty directions at once, constantly interrupted by pages and EMR messages. In the evenings, we chart at home, following up on those labs and studies we ordered earlier, while our families wait for us patiently. We know those working in the clinic have even more responsibilities for follow-up and coordination of care for their continuity panel of patients.

The problem is multifaceted. It's not just the frenetic stress of running through the day, barely catching our breath. It's not just the emotional drain of showing up for each patient and shouldering the burdens of their medical and social problems. Nor is it just the deep exhaustion of decision fatigue, a result of the hundreds of critical choices we make in a given clinical day.

A second layer of demands comes from the system beyond patient care. Administrators dictate the details of the delivery of patient care. There are metrics to be tracked and compliance training series to complete after hours and on the weekends. Insurance companies set up barriers and hoops to jump through when you prescribe medications, order therapy, and discharge a patient from the hospital to a nursing facility. Then there are the forms we fill out for everything, from DME to work excuses to L&I releases—not to mention the EMR, listed as one of the primary causes for the epidemic levels of burnout in the physician population.

On top of that, we experience disrespect for what we do from the general public, and often even our own patients. Some demand we do certain tests or provide medications based on what they were told by Dr. Google or advised by the latest online guru. We are called names when we explain why that testing isn't indicated, or why we do not think it is the best choice to prescribe opiates or antibiotics for a particular complaint. We are accused of not caring. Sometimes, we are even personally threatened.

ENTER THE PANDEMIC

The COVID-19 pandemic in 2020 only made the situation worse.

Many hospitals didn't have the PPE supplies that we needed to protect ourselves. We didn't know much about the virus or how contagious it was. We worried about getting sick.

We also worried about getting our families sick. Like many doctors, Kenji and I had a procedure for getting changed out of our scrubs in the garage to avoid contaminating our kids and each other. We carried antibacterial wipes in our cars and in the hospital. We wiped down computers before we touched them. And we sat far away from our colleagues in our team rooms.

One Texas-based emergency room doctor we know is a widow and single mom of two young kids. For the first eight months of the pandemic, she worked as many of her shifts back to back as she could while her kids stayed with their grandparents. She then quarantined before seeing them. Another doctor we know lived in a camper van in his backyard to avoid exposing his family to the virus.

How many of us did something similar?

While we feared for ourselves and our family and carried the burden of watching our patients die at alarming rates, we felt like we were on our own. We felt as if the hospital and system that was supposed to have our backs put us out to dry. They didn't have the supplies to protect us initially; and sometimes they didn't even let us use those supplies when they had them.

How many of us remember the days when we were allowed only one N95 a week, and how we carried it between patient rooms in a paper bag labeled with our names along with our goggles or face shield?

One doctor we knew advocated early on in the pandemic for the ability to wear a mask in the hospital at all times. Hospital administration told him he couldn't wear a mask outside of patient rooms because he'd scare the patients and families. Because he wanted to wear a mask whenever he was in the hospital, he felt his job was threatened. Ironically, just a month or two later, the public was advised to wear masks everywhere. Suddenly, when there were more supplies available, the recommendations changed.

Meanwhile, all of us in healthcare had walked around the hospital unmasked between caring for COVID patients. How many of us got sick or got other patients sick because of it?

Adding to the personal and familial stress, doctors faced the trauma of caring for a multitude of dying patients. We had family meetings over Zoom. We helped people say goodbye to their loved ones from afar.

All of this was compounded by the personal financial stress

brought by the pandemic. As hospitals shut down elective surgeries and other services, and primary care offices closed, doctors and their staff suffered financially. Hospitalists took pay cuts and missed out on bonuses due to lost revenue. As one family medicine doctor in Texas said: "I never worked harder to get paid less."

As doctors, we lined up to get our COVID vaccines as soon as possible in the fall of 2020—we didn't want to die, and we didn't want our family members or anyone in the general public to unnecessarily die either. Almost five months pregnant, I felt immensely relieved to get mine after working so long in the hospital unprotected. Yet, we still spent our days taking care of the unvaccinated, whose choices put us at more risk. Those who refused the vaccine did so due to a disbelief in science and a distrust of doctors and the medical community. This rubbed salt into our already-raw wounds. We toiled in the hospitals and clinics trying to help those who did not believe in the science-backed care we were delivering, and who disparaged us online and sometimes even in person—yet they still sought our care. The gravity of this experience on doctors and other healthcare professionals cannot be understated—and it will have repercussions for years to come.

No wonder many of us working on the inside question how medicine has gotten to this place and, even more critically, how long we will personally last in this current system.

The truth is most of us were led to practice medicine by our hearts and by our aspiration to serve others. Now we suffer under the yoke of the modern medical system, our ability to truly serve our patients stymied by a system steered for profit and a societal culture steeped in anti-science philosophy.

WHAT CAN BE DONE?

As many would suggest, doctors can work on themselves to help make the day-to-day more palatable and ultimately reduce burnout. We can get therapy and coaching, work on mindfulness, and practice yoga. That will certainly help. There's no doubt that when we empower ourselves to manage our minds, it makes a significant difference in the quality of our lives.

But what about the system?

Does the system get to continue its descent into a bureaucracy led by nonclinical experts? Does the system get to continue to make the rules of how patient care is delivered while doctors and medical staff are treated as dispensable cogs? Will there be no reckoning, no consequences, besides the litany of burned-out doctors strewn along the way?

Some of you may believe the trajectory of clinical medicine has already been decided. You may think that there is no hope.

You see how we doctors are currently splintered from one another. You see how we have been stripped of our power and autonomy. You see how we have tolerated the slow erosion of our control. You know we rely on our paychecks to support our families and to pay back the huge debt burdens we accumulated during our training, so we don't think we have a choice, besides putting our heads down and working harder.

But, for some of us, there is a glimmer of hope for change—and we believe that starts by taking back control through gaining financial independence from our clinical incomes.

What would happen if we didn't need our paychecks to survive and to support our families? How many of us would be willing to tolerate the erosion of autonomy, the climbing patient responsibility, and the administrative burden that has characterized our careers to this point? I suspect not many. In fact, many of us would stand up and demand change.

What would you do if you were financially free?

Maybe you would walk away. The fact is many of us would leave medicine tomorrow if we didn't need the paycheck. We would leave the broken system to protect ourselves and our families. We would do it out of personal survival.

Maybe you would choose to cut back. This was a decision I made once we were financially free. Half-time as a hospitalist made such a difference in my quality of life. It allowed me to be present for my family and enjoy my work at a different level. I was a better doctor because of it.

Or maybe you would turn to volunteering, practicing medicine the way you thought you would when you first decided to become a doctor. Maybe your contribution would be starting your own clinic, where you could treat your patients the way you felt was in their best interest, independent of finances. Or maybe you would take a lower-paying job at a place that delivered care in a way that really served the best interest of the patients.

If doctors had financial freedom, a crisis would likely result from what would surely be a mass exodus of doctors and other healthcare professionals. Patient care might initially suffer. Hospital and clinical system finances built on the backs of doctors always willing to do more[1] might even collapse.

But what if this cold reality and the resulting crisis would force the system to adapt and change? What if, out of the ashes, a new, improved system was forged?

To attract doctors who didn't rely on their paycheck to survive, this new medical system would be forced to create an environment where physicians were recognized and valued. The culture of medicine would need to make space for doctors and other medical professionals to be their best selves at work *and* at home. It would be sustainable to be a doctor again.

What would that even look like?

Well for starters, we doctors would demand the system focus on patient care first. Insurance and administrators would no longer dictate care. This would allow us to better care for our patients. We would also make the environment much more sustainable for ourselves. We would have a less exhausting workload. There would be strict boundaries—work would stay at work and not trail us home. We would not chart and follow up on labs on nights and weekends when we were supposed to be with our families. Our incomes would be high enough to pay off our student loans while providing for our families—even if we chose to be a pediatrician

---

1   Danielle Ofri, "The Business of Health Care Depends on Exploiting Doctors and Nurses," *The New York Times*, June 8, 2019. https://www.nytimes.com/2019/06/08/opinion/sunday/hospitals-doctors-nurses-burnout.html.

or primary care doctor. We would show up filled from within, with capacity to give and to serve the way we imagined we would when we put on our white coats for the very first time.

We would care for one another. We would connect at work again, not just rush by each other in the hallways with only a quick nod of acknowledgment. The doctors' lounge might even become that again—a lounge where doctors could revel in the joys of the day, discuss difficult cases together in person, or perhaps even take time to read medical journals. With community connections re-bound, perhaps those who are deeply suffering would be recognized and given the support they so desperately need before there were dire consequences.

Patients would be happier. Doctors would be happier. Burnout would decrease. The care delivered would improve. And the medical system would be sustainable for both doctors *and* patients.

Imagine that.

A MASS MOVEMENT

Does this sound like a pipe dream to you?

We admit, we can see how it would sound like a long shot. How could we ever get enough doctors and other medical professionals to be financially free enough to make a difference in the medical system?

It would take a *mass movement*—and that's what this book is about.

Kenji and I are part of a movement of doctors and healthcare professionals who are working toward no longer having to trade their time for money. There are thousands of us who have already achieved or are working toward financial freedom using real estate investments.

Our primary goal in writing this book is to continue this work and reach *even more* of our community who are dissatisfied and yearn for more, and show them that there is another way.

We want to help band even more doctors together in a common community so each of you can start to dream bigger for yourselves, your families, and the future. By doing this, we know that you will be empowered to change medicine from within.

Of all the people who can change medicine for the better, it's us—doctors and other medical workers—who are on the front lines and in the trenches. We engage in direct patient care. We see the holes and weaknesses of the system. We are the ones who came into the system with a dream of helping patients. As such, we have to be the ones to create the vision for how it can change for the better—and make that a reality.

We need to do it for ourselves, too, because now and in the future we and our loved ones will be patients.

When doctors lead, anything is possible. We are highly motivated, focused problem solvers. We are creative. We are driven by higher ideals. We want to contribute and serve. Imagine how much better the world would be if doctors used these unique characteristics to usher in reform and positive changes. It would truly be beautiful.

Why not take on the system? Why not mold it into something better?

You may be thinking, *That's impossible.* And you may be right. But in the face of uncertainty, we have two choices.

One: we can do nothing. If we do that, though, we abandon our colleagues, our patients, and the medical system. The culture of medicine and the U.S. healthcare system will continue down this unsustainable road, and the suffering will continue for all. Where it will end up twenty years from now is anyone's guess.

Or two: we can choose to dream this impossible dream together. And then we can go make it happen.

We prefer the latter.

Kenji and I believe that the first step to reforming the system is getting you and all our other colleagues financially free as fast as possible—so that you can make decisions from a place of abundance, not survival. So you have choices. So that you have the freedom to make the hard decisions that benefit your patients without sacrificing yourself. Fortunately, we know how to help you get that freedom through real estate investing.

WHY REAL ESTATE INVESTING?

As doctors writing to doctors, why are we telling you that investing in real estate is the solution?

Because it worked for us as a dual physician couple, it's worked for the thousands of doctors we've trained, and we know it can work for you, too.

Later in this book, we'll look more closely at why real estate investing is an optimal vehicle to financial independence and freedom for high-income-earning professionals like doctors. But there are a few fundamental ideas about real estate investing to set in your mind now as you continue reading and consider this journey for yourself through this book:

Owning income-producing rentals is the key to replacing your medical income. Investing in properties that bring in monthly cashflow is what will allow you to replace your clinical salary and achieve financial freedom long before retirement age.

Real estate investing offers immense tax benefits for doctors and high-income professionals. There are several ways you can shelter part or even all of your medical salary from taxes, boosting your retained earnings substantially.

Investing in certain types of estate is relatively downturn resistant. Economic ups and downs can be a huge deterrent for potential real estate investors, but we'll show you that when you choose the right types of properties, you can mitigate a lot of the risk involved when there is a downturn.

Real estate can be passive. You can be as involved as you want in your real estate investments, making this financial path perfect for someone with a career who is looking for more freedom in their life—not just more work. Your time is not directly tied to your returns when you invest in real estate.

The real estate investment community of like-minded doctors and high-income professionals is ready and waiting. You don't have to start from scratch with real estate. It's a path that is full of resources and experts prepared to help you throughout your journey. One of those resources is the Semi-Retired MD community, made up of thousands of doctors and high-income professionals who are already on the journey.

If it sounds like real estate investing could be a potential path for you, keep reading. There's no better way to visualize the journey you could be on than to read the story we're about to share with you.

To help you start making progress right away, you'll find a series of links to free downloads and resources throughout this book. Building a future of financial freedom starts with just a single step. By the time you finish this book, you will have made significant progress in getting closer to building a life of your dreams if you take advantage of some or all of the free resources included in the pages that follow.

LEARN MORE

Get a free download of our resource, "How to Make $100,000 in the First Year of Real Estate Investing" to get several examples of how you can make significant returns in just your first year of investing in real estate. Access the resource by visiting: semiretiredmd.com/life-100k.

ABOUT THIS BOOK

This book is built on a fictional journey of two doctors: Ben, who adheres to the path of conventional wisdom, and Maya, who decides she wants something more—and how she finds that through investing in income-producing rental properties. We will primarily follow Maya and her husband Jay's experience as they become real estate investors and eventually achieve financial freedom.

We chose to structure this book as a story because we believe telling stories is a more effective and engaging way to teach important concepts. We humans are by nature more invested when we hear a tale filled with human trials and tribulations as opposed to being fed a set of highly arranged facts. Our intention is to use story to help you to internalize the financial concepts introduced in this book and be able to remember them so you draw upon them when you make your own financial decisions down the road.

The downside of this book being built as a story is that it is a simplification of a doctor's financial journey through real estate investing. When you embark on the real estate investment path, unique complexities are bound to exist. Even though we couldn't cover all possible scenarios in this book, we aimed to provide you with a clear outline of what a journey to financial freedom through real estate can look like for a doctor or high-income professional like yourself. Through Maya and Jay's story, we aimed to show you what's possible, even though each of us will have our own separate path to walk.

Kenji and I also want to highlight that although this book is based on contrasts between the characters and their choices, it is not about judgment. As you read through the story, you are likely to identify with parts of both Maya's and Ben's journeys.

Be kind to yourself and to others as you read this fictional tale. We all have financial skeletons in the closet. Any and all mistakes you (and we) have made in the past are excellent learning opportunities, which force us to grow.

We truly believe we either **get the result we wanted or the lesson we needed**.

In this book, you will be introduced to a novel view of investing, one you've not been taught in medical school or through traditional financial dogma. Real estate investments, and specifically owning income-producing/cashflowing rental properties, can be a significant and transformative part of your investment portfolio. They can help you get to financial freedom long before traditional investments.

The good news: as you read this book, you'll be building your financial muscles and learning the steps in how to start investing in real estate. Perhaps by the end of it, maybe you'll even choose to take on an additional identity—that of a real estate investor.

We hope you recognize you've taken the first step by picking up *Life On Your Terms: Why Doctors Use Real Estate Investments to Set Themselves Free and How You Can Too*. You've started your journey to financial and time freedom. Congratulations on taking action! Use the momentum you gain from this book to continue moving forward, to help you build a life you love.

ABOUT US

While not a biography by any stretch of the imagination, the story of Maya and Jay is loosely based on Kenji's and my experiences as physician real estate investors. Over the course of seven years, we built a portfolio of long- and short-term rentals that currently spans more than 150+ units.

We've also sprinkled in some actual experiences from members of our community to make the story even more dramatic, engaging, and fun. Everyone loves a good hero's journey after all!

A bit about who we are: I (Leti) earned a medical degree from the University of Vermont and a master's in development anthropology from The George Washington University. After completing my residency in family medicine at Swedish Hospital in Seattle, I fell in love with hospital medicine and became a hospitalist. I worked as a hospitalist until late 2020—pregnant, in the middle of COVID, and overseeing a small team of employees as CEO of Semi-Retired MD, I made the extremely difficult decision to cut back in medicine in order to focus more on being a CEO, mother, wife, and real estate investor. In total, I was an employed hospitalist for ten years, working for Swedish Hospital, Good Samaritan Hospital, and Queen's Medical Center. At the time of this writing, Kenji and I have trained more than three thousand doctors and high-income professionals to invest in real estate through Semi-Retired MD and our online courses, *Zero to Freedom* and *Accelerating Wealth*, and our membership site, Empire Builders.

Kenji earned a medical degree from Johns Hopkins. After finishing his first internship, he left medicine and worked in the corporate world, including at McKinsey and Co., for about five years before returning to residency. After completing an internal medicine residency at the University of Washington, he worked as a hospitalist at Swedish Hospital for twelve years (where he met me). Kenji is a serial entrepreneur, having started his first business in medical school. In addition to our real estate portfolio, he has started several other multiple multimillion-dollar businesses in the healthcare space.

Prior to us investing together as a couple in 2015, Kenji owned rental properties and raw land from 2001. Although he gained valuable experience investing through multiple downturns, he made the mistake of investing heavily for appreciation, not cashflow, and got caught in 2008 with non-income-producing properties. This prior experience, combined with what we learned on our personal journey into real estate investing, has informed the development of the content for our Semi-Retired MD blog, podcast, courses, and other services.

As full-time hospitalists, Kenji and I both had thriving careers when we got together, but we knew at the pace we were going—like Kenji's doctor, Dr. Smith (whose name was changed to protect anonymity)—we were on the road to burnout.

It was so bad, in fact, that we had to schedule something we called LAKA Days—days we'd get to spend the whole day together, not working or attending to other life responsibilities—*a couple months* in advance. We didn't see things getting any better any time soon, either. We knew we wanted to build a family, and we wanted to travel, but with what our work schedules were at the time, we didn't know how that would happen without sacrificing our time together. This drove us to actively think about how we could achieve these future goals without being so dependent on our full-time doctor salaries.

We found the answer in owning income-producing rental properties—our ticket to financial freedom.

On a trip to New Zealand (much like this story's heroes, Maya and Jay), we read Robert Kiyosaki's *Rich Dad Poor Dad* and completely changed our path. We realized if we could get enough monthly cashflow/income through real estate investments, then we wouldn't need to depend solely on our doctor salaries anymore, and we wouldn't need to wait until we were sixty-five to have time freedom for each other and the future children we desired. We could practice medicine and live *life on our own terms*—and maybe even buy and spend time in a property in Italy we daydreamed about. We'd also be much better positioned to financially weather anything that might happen to us along the way—whether it was medical illness or job loss or needing to spend more time with aging parents. We would never have to be beholden to anyone else for our financial security.

We would be able to do what we wanted, when we wanted, with whom we wanted.

Kenji and I spent the next few years diving into real estate investing, building our rental portfolio, learning the ins and outs of harvesting tax benefits and running rehabs, making mistakes and learning from them, and growing. What started with a couple duplexes and a fourplex during year one grew over time as we poured all our energy, savings, earnings, and tax refunds into buying more investment properties. Similar to Jay in our story, Kenji cut back to half-time and then to moonlighting to maximize our tax savings using real estate professional status (REPS), which you will learn about in the pages that follow.

By the end of 2018, we had achieved financial freedom—meaning we had reached the point where we could survive on our real estate income alone. Since then, we've dedicated our lives to helping other doctors like us do the same.

LEARN MORE

Want to learn the exact method we used to get to financial freedom so quickly? We share the details in our blog on the Fast FIRE System at semiretiredmd.com/life-fastfire.

Kenji and I launched the Semi-Retired MD blog in 2018 to help our friends and colleagues learn how to apply the Fast FIRE System, the roadmap for how we achieved financial freedom so quickly using real estate, for themselves. Starting in 2019, we developed a series of courses, including *Zero to Freedom* and *Accelerating Wealth*, which provide doctors with all the knowledge they need to go from knowing nothing about real estate to buying their first cashflowing property.

Our courses, membership site, and everything else we do is driven by the mission of our business: to help empower doctors and their families to use real estate investments to build lives they love. Some of the experiences from our students will give you an idea of what's possible for you:

Larry, a radiation oncologist living in Alaska with his wife, Prairie, set out toward his dream of building enough real estate income so that he didn't have to rely on his medical income. He wanted his work as an oncologist to be his contribution to the world. Less than three years after taking *Zero to Freedom*, he completely replaced his clinical income with real estate cashflow. He's now working half-time, climbing, learning to fly, and spending more time with his family.

Jennifer and Rafal are a dual doctor couple in Maine who were burned out. Through real estate, they created $120,000 in cashflow in nine months, which allowed Jennifer to leave her family medicine job and pursue her dream of running her own medi-spa. Without having to depend on his salary anymore, Rafal switched jobs that gave him more time on weekends to spend with their young children. Less than two years after taking *Zero to Freedom*, they have more than sixty units of long- and short-term rentals.

Mike is the family medicine doctor we introduced earlier, who took a pay cut during the pandemic. He and his wife, Renee, live in Austin, Texas. According to Mike, "[Real estate] reignited my passion for medicine in a way that I didn't anticipate." Before, he felt like he was tied to a W-2 job. Now, he's enjoying his work, taking more patients, and feels liberated. He actually enjoys practicing family medicine again.

Jessica is the emergency room doctor in Texas who had to leave her kids with her parents for extended periods of time during the height of the pandemic. Since then, as a single mother, Jessica has built a portfolio with nineteen long- and short-term rental doors and has become a syndicator involved in overseeing hundreds of units, enabling her to cut back at work and spend more time with her kids. She's an inspiring example of how you can do this, even by yourself.

Alisa earned multiple hundreds of thousands of dollars per

year in real estate cashflow within two years of taking the *Zero to Freedom* course by investing in and self-managing short-term and long-term rentals. She embarked on this journey herself—her husband wasn't interested in participating—while working full-time as a GI doctor and raising four kids. With her newfound financial independence, Alisa is now planning new adventures, including climbing Mt. Kilimanjaro.

While each of our students is unique, they all have one thing in common: They're **using income-producing rental properties to live their lives on their terms.**

LIFE ON YOUR TERMS

This book is dedicated to you—the doctors and high-income professionals who dare to step outside of the traditional path set before them to make their dreams a reality. Building wealth through real estate takes effort, focus, and persistence. It takes grit and dreaming. It's choosing to aim high instead of playing small and safe. It means tackling challenges head-on and pursuing a better future for yourself, your family, and the world—no matter what.

Once you learn how to invest in income-producing properties, the skills you will gain will set you free—and that's when you can live *life on your terms.*

In our story that follows, you will see how Maya and Jay use real estate as the vehicle to start **living their life on their terms.**

Through their journey, you will learn:

- Why they, as doctors, longed for something more for themselves and their family.
- How they discovered real estate investing and why they decided it was the right financial path for them.
- The doubts, limiting beliefs, challenges they had to overcome.
- The education they invested in to gain the knowledge they needed.
- The choices they made as they built their real estate portfolio.
- How they put in the work to build generational wealth and contribute to something outside of themselves.

Through this book, you will follow their path as they realize a different life—a life they love.

Then you'll see how it's possible for *you* to do it, too.

CHAPTER 1

MEET THE DOCS

"You're already a financial trader. You might not think of it this way, but if you work for a living, you're trading your time for money. Frankly, it's just about the worst trade you can make. Why? You can always get more money, but you can't get more time."

—TONY ROBBINS

"Hey there, nice bike outside. I noticed it when you pulled up. I'm Ben, by the way."

"Maya," the woman smiled, introducing herself. "And thanks. I'm hoping to do more biking around the city to explore. I don't know Seattle very well yet. Today's my first day as an internal med intern."

"Hey, me too! We must be in the same program!" Ben said. "And I bike as well. Maybe we can ride together sometime... So, first day of residency. Are you nervous?"

"A little," Maya said. "It's actually not my first go-around at residency. I left my first program for a different job. But I'm back and ready now to make a difference in my patients' lives."

"Yeah, me too," said Ben with an eager smile. "It's been a journey to get here, but I'm stoked to step closer to having my own patients to care for." Ben, like most doctors, was driven to serve his patients. He was sure residency would be a wild ride the next few years, but he was ready, too.

It'd be good to have a friend.

MEET MAYA

Maya's dad, Tomás, was a doctor. He was a first-generation physician who moved from Argentina to the United States to provide a better opportunity for his work and for his kids. He worked hard and was recognized as a devoted doctor by the medical community at his retirement. Tomás spent the bulk of his life working for the same academic hospital, following the time-honored path to professorship. He valued loyalty and consistency. Medicine and the ideal of being an "excellent doctor" drove his professional pursuits.

As a result, Maya's father was largely absent from home. He was always toiling away in his lab or teaching medical students. His profession—his calling—came first.

When he was present, Tomás made sure that his children were lectured on the value of hard work, getting a good education, and securing a stable job. He wanted things to be easier for them than they had been for his parents and his family. He wanted his kids to have the security to never have to worry about finances. He valued having a reliable job.

Maya didn't always follow the traditional path her father had laid out. Sure, she was pre-med in college. She spent summers in the medical research lab helping him out while building her CV. But she had also veered off the path. In fact, she had veered way off the path, as far as her father was concerned.

Maya was involved in a start-up during medical school. It didn't go anywhere, and after a year of working effectively for free, she left the company with little to show for her effort and time. That was definitely not the path to financial stability and educational achievement in Tomás's mind.

Maya went back to medicine, but just when her father thought she was back on track, she wildly veered off again to work in financial consulting, having not even finished her internal medicine residency program! Tomás was not impressed. He worried that his daughter was unfocused and had unrealistic expectations for her life.

After several years of work in the pressure cooker of Wall Street, Maya finally made it back to medicine and was beginning residency again. Her dad was proud and, honestly, incredibly relieved. She was finally on track. Maya would have a stable, reliable job. She would settle down, get married, and have a family. She'd start to build her clinical knowledge and publish academic journals. She'd move to leadership positions in the hospital over time. She'd be well-respected by the community. Everything was as he thought it should be.

While things appeared on track to Tomás, however, Maya was fascinated by solving problems using an out-of-the-box approach. She was always looking for the next opportunity to make things better—including in her own life. She was not destined to follow the traditional route for long.

MEET BEN

Ben, like Maya, was raised by a family who valued hard work. His parents ran a successful grocery store business in their small town in central New York. As much as he loved helping his family in the business when he was child, over time it lost its appeal, especially as he saw how much it took out of them.

Ben saw his parents go through financial struggles over the years. They often worked weekends to keep their business afloat by minimizing expenses to make ends meet. This meant Ben's parents were preoccupied while he was young, and he was mostly raised by his grandmother.

Luckily, Ben's grandmother was an energetic woman who could keep up with young Ben and his older sister. She believed in the value of getting a good education. She hovered over their homework starting even in kindergarten, correcting his spelling and handwriting with a meticulous eye. She kept the kids on the right track, as far as Ben's parents were and she was concerned, anyway.

Ben and his sister grew up hearing they only had three career choices: they could be doctors, lawyers, or engineers. It was a given that they'd be attending college and then pursuing an advanced degree after that.

As Ben entered high school, his parents' grocery business really took off, becoming hugely profitable. This gave him a firsthand view of how a successful business could create resources for its entrepreneurial owners.

Nevertheless, Ben's parents and grandmother continued to guide him toward getting a "good" education and securing a stable career over entrepreneurship. The family didn't want him to be at the mercy of the uncertainty that they had to endure as business owners. They also didn't want him to have to sacrifice his life outside of work, like they had, to get to where they were. They didn't realize that going into a "stable job" could also have that same consequence.

Of the three choices he was presented with, Ben decided medicine suited him best. He liked helping people. He didn't mind the sight of blood, and he was good at chemistry. Ben attended the local state college as a pre-med and when he excelled in the basic sciences, Ben and his family assumed he would go on to medical school at the state university. When he was accepted to an Ivy League program, however, everyone was beyond thrilled. Ben was living up to his family's expectations of him. Everything was going according to the plans his parents and grandmother had drilled into him for so many years.

Despite heavy competition, Ben worked hard and consistently scored at the top of his class at one of the premier medical schools. His laser focus remained on two goals: becoming a stellar, well-recognized physician and making his family proud.

At the end of his third year, Ben settled on applying for residency in internal medicine, as a path to neurology or perhaps even hematology. He was accepted into a well-respected internal medicine residency program in Seattle. The first day, he met Maya.

A FRIENDSHIP IS BORN

Over the next three years as residents, Ben and Maya built the type of enduring bond that only comes from struggling through thirty-six-hour shifts, being abused by bitter attendings, and scarfing down midnight burgers and chocolate shakes from the hospital cafeteria at 3 a.m.

In their third year of residency, Ben and Maya both decided to get jobs as hospitalists when they graduated. For Ben, it was a short-term play: he wanted to earn some cash while he applied to a fellowship in hematology. He'd pay down his student loans while finding his fellowship of choice. He also felt like he had deferred living his life for enough time, and he needed a short break before jumping back into the fire of being a trainee again.

For Maya, being a hospitalist was the natural choice. She liked the fast-paced hospital, where she had a chance to work with a range of patients. She liked working in the ICU. She also didn't want to deal with the rote schedules or paperwork she saw burying her colleagues in the clinic. Hospitalist work would give her a little more freedom to decide when she saw her patients and how long she spent with them. Finally, she valued her work/life balance. Entering the workforce as an older doctor (after her time on Wall Street), she was ready to start making real money and living her life.

Maya and Ben were lucky enough to both secure jobs at the local community hospital. They were well-paid positions, and their schedules were one week on, one week off. Ben would have the time to apply to fellowship and build out his résumé. Maya would have the time to explore her hobbies and ride her bike.

All their lives, Maya and Ben had been working toward this moment: becoming attending physicians. And it had finally, *finally* arrived.

"Hey," said Ben, jogging to catch up with Maya on their last hospital shift as residents. "Well, last day as a resident, how does it feel?"

"Such a relief!" exclaimed Maya. "Just think, starting Monday, we're in the driver's seat. No more Q4 calls. No more pimping!" she said with a deep exhale. Pimping had always given Maya serious anxiety.

"Yep, and we don't have to deal with Dr. Negative Nancy or Dr. Toxic Tony changing our care plans—or overruling them," said Ben. These were their code names for the difficult attendees they'd worked with the past few years.

Maya and Ben knew these doctors were this way because of the stress of their jobs. They were tired, and it made them angry. Still, they could just be straight-up cruel at times, even in front of patients. They had seen other residents crying after particularly difficult morning rounds. And, even if they didn't want to admit it, they had felt that way frequently too. It had been a challenging three years.

"And no more dealing with Dr. Lee's bad moods and running an hour behind in clinic," Maya added. "We're hospitalist attendings now!"

"Although I will miss Dr. Jacobs, I learned a ton from her," Ben said. "She said she'll write me a recommendation when I apply for fellowship programs."

Maya smiled. "I'm just so excited to finally use all my training to do things the way I think they should be done to help my patients. I want to help them change and not get readmitted every month. I want to teach them to have a better quality of life. And to transition more smoothly at the end of life. I'm going to spend a lot more time doing that. Ben, I mean, this is why we became doctors!"

"I know," said Ben. "And I'm sure we're going to continue to see some really interesting cases as the hospital grows to become a bigger referral center, too. I can't wait to swap stories as we learn and see more over the next couple of years.

"Not to mention," he continued. "We can start living our lives again! Remember those bike rides we talked about on our first day? To go explore Seattle? We actually can do that now!" They were overjoyed.

They'd made it through three rough years of residency. Sure, they'd found themselves grumbling or getting irrationally angry at little things on a daily basis by six months in. They may have even cursed at their pagers and joked about dropping them out the third-story call room windows. But now that *they* were attendings, things were going to be different. They were in charge. They were in control of their time. They would get to choose how to care for patients. They would educate them, help them get better, and connect with their families at the bedside.

They were finally starting their lives as real doctors. And it was going to be awesome!

THE COST OF MEDICAL EDUCATION

As Maya and Ben began their roles as hospitalists, a new financial reality quickly set in: payments were starting on their student debt, which had ballooned over their years of training.

"Man, I'm really thankful to be working now," Maya said. "I need to start paying off my student loans soon. I can't believe how much my loans grew over the last seven years because of that interest."

During residency, Maya had married the love of her life and fellow doctor, Jay. Between the two of them, they had nearly $400,000 in student loan debt. Ben was $150,000 in the hole for his medical education. His wife, Jenna, a college professor, thankfully didn't have student loans to worry about.

"I know," said Ben. "But just think, we're actually better off than most—I read the other day the average medical school grad has more than $240,000 in total student loan debt. Neither of us have quite that amount just by ourselves."

"Still," said Maya. "Remember that financial planner they brought in to talk to us during residency? That was his no. 1

message: debt is bad. We need to get these loans paid off as soon as possible." Neither Ben nor Maya were quite at a point where they wanted to pay for their own private financial advisors, but they certainly would take the advice of one sponsored by the hospital.

"Jay and I have a plan to get our debt paid off as quickly as we can," Maya continued. "We're going to be aggressive about it and pay as much as we can each month toward the loans. Even though we won't be building up much in savings."

"Wow, that's great," said Ben. "Jenna and I have been wanting to buy a house soon, so I've been taking more of the pay-the-minimum-balance approach, you know? I figure, student loans have such a low interest rate—it's not like it's credit card debt—so we can take a bit more time. Plus, I'm maxing out my contributions to my 401(k) to make sure I get the hospital's 3 percent match. That's what the financial advisor said to do, right?"

"He sure did," said Maya. She was doing the same. "I mean, with that 3 percent match, someday we'll retire comfortably."

"Yeah, like when we're eighty," Ben said sarcastically.

With their new jobs as hospitalists, Ben and Maya's financial decisions felt heftier, but following the conventional advice provided to them by the financial advisors brought in by their residency director seemed like the wise move.

They'd worked hard to get where they were and were proud of the work they were doing. With new jobs and decent salaries, they looked forward to what the next years would bring as they stopped having to live in delayed gratification and finally started living real lives.

After all, they had seen their friends from college have money—and spend it on houses, cars, and trips—for years. Ben was in his late twenties and Maya in her early thirties. Yet, they had nothing to show but debt from years of education.

It was time to start living.

CHAPTER 2

LIFE AS HOSPITALISTS

"...As you get older, your toys get more expensive—a new car, a boat and a big house to impress your friends... Fear pushes you out the door, and desire calls to you. That's the trap."

—ROBERT KIYOSAKI

"Hey there," said Ben. "So, what ya got for me this week?"

Maya was finishing up her latest hospitalist shift and doing her weekly phone call handoff to Ben. The reality of being an attending physician had taken a couple years to sink in, but by the end of their second year, they were both exhausted.

During their handoff chats between shifts, they leaned on each other, trading sarcastic jokes and commiserating with each other about patients, the system, nurses, and others. Cynicism helped them cope.

"Well, I have some notes here," said Maya, tiredly. "818 is ready to be discharged tomorrow when you take over. I'm relieved she's going to go home. I thought she'd end up in a SNF, so that's good news. I left her discharge note for you. I've reconciled her meds."

"612, Mrs. Howard, is back in again this week—with cellulitis. We told her she needs to get her A1C down and lose some weight, but she doesn't seem to get it. And 546 is also a bounce back, with a CHF exacerbation. He stopped taking his Lasix when he ran out of pills last week. His wife doesn't drive, so they couldn't find a way to pick up his new prescription." Maya took a deep breath, and then continued. "No interesting cases, just the usual. It's all there." Maya rubbed the back of her neck, sore from days of wearing her stethoscope and hunching over the computers. She was spent.

"Oh, and do you remember Ms. Frank? That sweet lady with a glioblastoma? How somebody with brain cancer can still care so much about everyone else around her, I'll never know. She's an absolute pleasure to see every day. She's in room 524, finishing up her FaceTime date with her husband. Thank God for her this week, Ben. She was a light I really, really needed."

"Yeah, it's been a rough past couple months," said Ben.

"Um, try a rough past couple *years*. Five days this week, I ate my lunch in the elevator," Maya said, shaking her head. "Scarfed it down in literally thirty seconds between floors. There's no time to talk or even take time to drink water! It's just go-go-go."

"And the thing is that when I finally finish a shift, I'm so tired, it takes me days to recover. *Days*," she continued, feeling defeated. "I can't wait to get out of here and sleep. I haven't biked in ages. We *still* haven't taken our bikes out to explore Seattle, and how long have we been here now?"

"Yep, I get it," said Ben. "I mean, I'm so excited to get in there tomorrow to start yet another week," he said sarcastically. "How'd you fare in the burnout training last week? I was moderate in everything."

As one of the hospital's many requirements, all hospital employees were required to complete a one-hour online session on how to combat burnout. It involved taking the Maslach Burnout Inventory test to assess doctor occupational burnout in three areas—emotional exhaustion, depersonalization, and personal accomplishment. They were scored on a scale of low, moderate, and high.

"I was high on depersonalization and exhaustion," said Maya. "Moderate in personal accomplishment, which makes sense, I guess. I feel like I'm not connecting with my patients or their families the way I used to or want to. Patients are starting to feel like just numbers on my list, a never-ending cycle of numbers. Even when I do get a zebra case, the fun of that is gone."

Both Maya and Ben had come to see hospital medicine as just a "Band-Aid" for patients. Patients bounced in and out of the hospital. Their health infrequently truly got better. Ben and Maya had started to believe that what they did made very little difference at all. The reality was they spent far more time with the computer and on notes than they ever did with patients. No wonder they were scoring high on the test. They had all the symptoms of burnout.

"Sometimes I wonder why I even got a medical degree," Ben added. "All I'm doing is admitting and discharging, admitting and discharging. I feel more like a paper pusher than I do a doctor. And my patients aren't even improving their health for the long term. They leave just to bounce back a couple of months later."

"The only thing that keeps me going is the few people I feel like I *actually* help," said Maya. "Like, Ms. Frank and Mr. Rizzo—you know, the patient with lung cancer? He died on Wednesday. I do think we helped him and his family do it in a way that was peaceful. But I feel like those moments are getting sparser. It's draining me."

"And you know what I really loved about that burnout training?" asked Ben. "That they somehow made me feel like it's my fault. My problem to fix. That I should just do some yoga. But do you see anything about the hospital changing? Nope. They just continue to pile more and more on us and think that we're just going to take it on. No wonder we're burned out!"

Their jobs had become more and more structured around the administration's latest metrics. Now their bonuses were paid depending on the number of patients they saw and the acuity of their illness (on RVUs). Even though they had no control over the patient numbers or acuity as hospitalists, it now partially determined their pay. As a hospitalist group, they were being encouraged to take on larger and larger loads with a smaller team in order to meet their numbers and get their full bonus.

"The hospital says I should now see eighteen patients a day. But you know how many I saw yesterday? Twenty-one," Maya said.

"Three came in after midnight, so they didn't even count them toward my RVUs. It feels like I'm on a treadmill and somebody just keeps pushing the speed up and up and up. And I just have to keep running, and I have no control. It's infuriating."

"Oh c'mon, but remember during the peak of COVID? We saw, what? Thirty patients a day? *And* they said they were taking our bonuses away. So twenty-one is nothing," Ben said, obviously joking, although they both knew their struggles were affecting them in very serious ways.

"Have you applied to any fellowships?" asked Maya. It had been Ben's plan all along to only work as a hospitalist for a few years, make some money, and then apply to fellowship, likely hematology.

"I decided I'm not going to do it," Ben said flatly. "What's the point? I see how hard the heme-onc doctors are working. Going back to low pay for several years of training, just to work more afterward? And juggling both clinic and hospital calls does not appeal *at all.* Why would I go through even more training, reduce my salary for a few years so I can't keep up on my student loan repayment schedule, and continue to kill myself working just as hard for no additional gain? I'm already working harder than when I was a resident. I can't do any more than I already am."

"Only now that we aren't in residency," Maya added, "instead of being at the whim of attendings, we're at the whim of the administrators."

It was true. The focus of their jobs had become more about the business side of medicine than patient care. The thrill of medicine had diminished for both of them. It had been replaced by a cruel reality.

"Well, try to have a good week off. Meanwhile, for me, this just might be the shift that this pager literally jumps right off me and slams itself to the ground," Ben said, smiling a half-hearted smile into the phone.

Maya hung up the phone and walked out of the hospital. She felt a huge sense of relief leaving.

THE OFF WEEKS

To Ben and Maya, it seemed like a new online training was added to their off weeks every year. These weren't within the scope of clinical work, they were additional hours stolen from their off week that they now spent completing in-person or online modules on anything the hospital deemed fit.

Plus they still had CME requirements to fulfill and significant medical licensing training requirements for their board and other certifications each year. One time, Ben had tried to calculate the numbers and was crushed to report he spent an additional 100 hours a year in just licensing, CME, and training requirements.

To make matters worse, this wasn't the only thing eating into his time off. In fact, more and more, all hospitalists' "off weeks" were eroding into more clinical work.

For one, the administration now required all doctors to join at least one hospital committee. Ben found himself attending biweekly pharmacy meetings at 7:00 a.m. on his off weeks. Maya was part of the culture of care committee. This didn't feel like the best use of their time, but it was required to show that they were good team members.

Hospital leadership was also debating whether hospitalists should follow up labs in their off weeks and call patients who they had recently discharged to check on their status at home. This would improve patient care, they thought. But what about caring for the doctors? It seemed that the medical staff's balance and health was not taken into account.

It was clear where things were going—and it wasn't up. Off weeks felt like they were turning into on weeks.

Everyone around them was working just as hard. Turnover was high as unhappy clinicians fled in search of better alternatives elsewhere, hoping they could find another job that offered more autonomy, a less heavy patient load, and an administration that didn't pay lip service to caring about their doctors. As a result, the hospital was always understaffed, and Ben and Maya were forced to pick up extra patients to cover team positions that could not be filled.

The specialists were also understaffed and suffering. The neurology team had to reduce coverage at the hospital to cover their responsibilities at other locations. The cardiologists were covering the hospital, heading into a full day of clinic, and then coming back to the hospital at the end of the day to finish consults. The psychiatrists were doing tele-psych for three different hospitals at once. The surgery group was fired en masse by administration and was replaced by those who had recently graduated from fellowship—because they were cheaper, of course.

"The oncologists are struggling," Maya had told Ben at one of their recent handoffs. "They're seeing patients in the morning in the hospital, then they're going to clinic, then they're getting consults during the day. And then they're coming back into the hospital at night. I saw Dr. DeBruin last night writing notes at 10:00 p.m. And Dr. James, one of the infectious disease docs? I overheard her say she has forty-five new consults today. Forty-five!"

Doctors in the hospital weren't connected to each other—they didn't have time to talk about shared patients, let alone get to know one another. They only communicated through their daily notes. This bred a culture of stress and survival in the hospital, rather than one of teamwork, growth, or improvement. No one understood the other's realities, which led to pointless infighting and negative interactions. Empathy for each other was hard to come by when all the doctors were drowning themselves.

Ben was definitely feeling the effects of that, he thought to himself, especially with everything going on in his personal life. That was on his mind as he strolled into the latest coding and billing training and plopped into the seat next to Maya.

"Well, hey there," Maya said. "I bet you're happy to be here on your day off."

Ben let out a sigh.

"How's Jenna? When is she due again?"

"She's doing well, due in January. She just wants to get moved into the lake house and be settled before the baby gets here. We're scheduled to close on the house in a few weeks."

Ben had big dreams for the life he wanted to provide for his new son and his wife, and that included a lake house for which they were currently under contract.

Ben did, however, already have some expenses that would make keeping up with the cost of a lake house a struggle. His first year as an attending, he had purchased a brand new yellow Porsche. It was the car of his dreams, and he loved driving it. He had been picking up two extra shifts for the last two years to make sure he paid it off quickly, but he still had a bit more to go.

Ben pulled out his phone and began showing Maya pictures of the house he and Jenna were buying.

"Check it out. A four-bedroom lake house with one-hundred-fifty feet of frontage," Ben said as he scrolled through the pictures. "Beautiful walk-in closet in the master for Jenna to store all those shoes she loves so much. And a wine cellar in the basement." Ben loved showering Jenna with gifts like wine, and neither of them had inexpensive taste.

"That's really beautiful, Ben," said Maya, pouring over the pictures. It would have been easy for her to be envious. It *was* a beautiful home. "Jay and I are more than a month into our home search. We've put in offers on three different houses so far, but we've been outbid every time."

Maya's husband, Jay, was a family medicine doctor who loved his work at the community health center. Like all clinicians, he was extremely busy managing patients in his clinic, while also following up on labs and doing paperwork after hours. Maya and Jay were both juggling full-time jobs. Squeezing in time together wasn't always easy.

They had a similar amount of money coming in each month as Ben and Jenna, but they had budgeted to buy a house roughly half of what Ben was spending on his lake house. Even though their lender told them they could "afford" more, they didn't want to feel "house-poor." It was one of several choices that would hopefully help set them up well in the future.

Maya and Jay both owned used cars they had bought in medical school and decided not to replace, for example. As a result, they didn't have monthly payments like Ben did on his Porsche.

They had also made the decision to live in a cheaper area outside of town so that they could put a few thousand dollars more toward their student loan payments each month. Though they had been paying them off aggressively for the last few years, they still had more than $250,000 left. They were on track to pay the balance off in five years.

Maya and Jay, too, were thinking about having kids and putting down their roots once they found the right house. They planned to use the small nest egg they'd saved for the down payment—if they ever could get an accepted offer, that is.

"I mean, for us, the monthly mortgage will be a stretch, but it's what Jenna and I have always wanted: to have a large family in the house of our dreams," said Ben. "I also want Jenna to cut back and work less once the baby comes if she wants. But we'll still need a nanny or preschool, so she can continue working some. That won't be cheap. We're also already thinking about private schools for the baby once he's older."

Ben knew all of these expenses came with a lot of responsibility—and money. But he was *finally* starting to live his life. After years of deferring spending in medical school and living lean during residency, on top of watching friends in other fields make money and buy nice things, he could finally reap the rewards of his career choice. He, too, deserved to buy nice things.

Even though he had bought the Porsche and lake house, Ben was also implementing some of the financial strategies he had been taught to secure his and his family's future.

He was saving for retirement in an effort to lower his taxes and secure his future. He and his wife were maximizing their 401(k) s. They were faithfully putting money in their HSAs. Though they hadn't had enough to fund their 457(b) yet, once he paid off his student loans in two more years, they'd be able to free up some funds for that, too. Plus, he only had $100,000 left in student loans after paying off five figures. They were going to start a 529 for their son in a couple of years. They were on the right track, at least according to what the financial advisors had advised. They took comfort in knowing they were going to have a comfortable retirement in thirty to forty years.

"With everything going on with us, with the new house and the baby, I'm going to need to pick up some moonlighting shifts to cover some of these additional monthly costs," Ben said. He looked anxious.

Maya looked at him, concerned. Ben was already working a full-time job, doing sixteen shifts a month. He had added an extra two to cover his Porsche payments. He needed to add three more shifts a month to make sure he could cover the new mortgage. That was twenty-one days of twelve-hour shifts a month. As it was, they spent their off weeks recovering. How was he ever going to get to de-stress if he was working all the time?

"It's just temporary," said Ben. "I'll manage. It's not even as much as what I worked in residency. I just need to power through for a couple of years until we can get my student loans paid off. Then I can cut back to full time. Jenna agrees. It's the only way to cover everything right now."

"I'm just worried about you, Ben," Maya responded. "I can see how exhausted you are already. I'm concerned you're not going to have enough recovery time between shifts working a schedule like this."

Ben appreciated her concern. But he didn't have a choice. The only way he saw to give his family the life they deserved was to put his head down and work harder—even if it meant doing more and more on his "off" weeks, which became increasingly rare.

He stuck to his plan.

EXTRA SHIFTS

Maya saw Ben hobbling down the hallway toward her. She had come into the hospital for a swing shift and was taking over from Ben, who was the day admitter. He looked horrible.

"Hey Ben," said Maya. "You're not looking too good. Did you do something to your back?"

"Yeah, I think it's just been the extra shifts I've been picking up lately," said Ben, rubbing his lower back. "I've been on my feet a lot and sleeping here at the hospital sometimes when I'm too tired to go home. Man, those call room beds suck. They are entirely uncomfortable."

"Geez, maybe you should lay off the moonlighting a bit," said Maya. "Or, here, do you need a pair of these?" Jokingly, she held out her foot to show him her new Danskos—literally the ugliest shoes ever. She'd refused to buy them for years, but now that she was solidly in her mid-thirties, her body was definitely feeling the physical impact of her job, and she had given in. She had even added some blue and yellow polka-dotted compression stockings to the mix—though at least those were halfway decent looking.

Her new Danskos were comfortable and handy, she admitted. She could just wipe them down and leave them in the garage when she got home. You couldn't see blood or any other fluids on them, for that matter. And, as a bonus, they even added an inch to her height! Though, sometimes, she must admit she tripped on them walking in the hallways due to the lift.

She could only imagine what Ben's feet and back felt like after all the hours he'd been working. She knew he felt the weight of his family and his finances on his shoulders.

"Well, walk me through the pending ER admissions so you can get out of here," she said. She wasn't happy to be there, but he needed to get home and rest.

"I'm sorry, I'm leaving you five in the ED. I got backed up with an ICU transfer, several consults, and then my day shift doctors were capped. I'm just so tired," Ben said.

Maya couldn't help but be annoyed. This really put her in a bind. It'd make the start to her shift much more stressful. She silently cursed that her hospitalist administration still didn't have a backup position to come in and help when there were days like this. But she knew why they didn't prioritize hiring a position like that: because it wouldn't add to their bottom line.

On a few previous occasions, Maya was told that hospitalists like herself and Ben were a cost center to the hospital—that they didn't make the hospital money and that only specialists did. Those words were painful to hear—and she had unfortunately heard them several times over the last couple of years.

Wow, Maya thought at the time. *I cost the hospital money?* It made her feel like the time, energy, and care she consistently brought to work wasn't valued or appreciated. No one should feel like that. No wonder the hospital didn't want to bring on an additional hospitalist salary.

Not having a backup position to help alleviate the load wasn't just horrible for her and Ben, either. It was bad for patients, too. They would endure longer waiting times in the ER. They would get rushed care. The nurses would get patients showing up on the floor without orders. There were consequential events down the chain from the patient to the doctors and medical staff.

Why didn't the administrators see that a few dollars spent on adequate staffing resulted in fewer patient care mistakes, less staff stress, and, ultimately, reduced longevity of their medical staff? It was a question Maya and Ben sometimes wondered out loud. Then again, maybe they did see, but they didn't care, because a dollar saved now was more important.

"I'm really sorry," said Ben. "But I was paged like twenty times this hour. I was just constantly interrupted." You could hear the stress in his voice. On top of that, Jenna had texted him a video during the shift of his son, Toby, now five months old, starting to roll over by himself. Not that Ben could even fathom being there for something like that—he was always here, at the hospital, just trying to make enough money to fund their life.

"Yeah, alright," said Maya. "I got it from here."

"Thanks," said Ben, apologetically. "Hey, any luck in the house search?" It'd been well over a year and Maya and Jay still hadn't found a house.

"Nope," said Maya. "We just put in another offer this morning, waiting to hear back. I don't have my hopes up."

"Well, good luck," said Ben, as he hobbled away. God, his back hurt.

"Thanks," said Maya, not even looking up from the computer screen. She was drudgingly starting yet another shift, and it already wasn't off to a good start.

CHAPTER 3

IT WAS ONLY A MATTER OF TIME

"If doctors and nurses clocked out when their paid hours were finished, the effect on patients would be calamitous. Doctors and nurses know this, which is why they don't shirk. The system knows it, too, and takes advantage."

—DR. DANIELLE OFRI

TRIGGER WARNING: This chapter contains content related to death by suicide. If you're struggling with thoughts of suicide, please reach out to the National Suicide Prevention Lifeline, 800-273-8255.

Authors' Note: Kenji and I lost two colleagues in our hospital to suicide in a single year. Their deaths greatly affected us and all the members of our hospitalist team. We struggled with whether or not to include suicide in this chapter, but ultimately decided that it needed to be in here. This is the reality of modern day medicine, and we included it not only to draw attention to how this is a real problem that affects all doctors, medical staff, patients, and families, but also to highlight how poorly hospital systems often handle such devastating situations.

We encourage anyone who is struggling to seek help. In addition to the Suicide Hotline, there's also a Physician Support Line where doctors volunteer their time to counsel other doctors and medical students. That number is 888-409-0141. It's free and confidential, with no appointment necessary, open seven days a week from 8:00 a.m. to 12:00 a.m. Eastern Time. For more information, visit www.physiciansupportline.com.

For those who want to learn more, we also recommend watching the documentary by Robyn Symon, *Do No Harm: Exposing the Hippocratic Hoax*. For more information, visit www.donoharm-film.com.

It was only a matter of time before it happened.

"Hey, did you hear about Tim?" Maya asked Ben on their hand-off call.

Tim was a hospitalist in their group. He'd worked there for seven years, and Ben and Maya had worked with him since they started nearly four years before.

Tim was one of the best doctors they had ever encountered, and they looked up to him immensely. He wasn't like the other more senior doctors who gave new doctors in the hospital a hard time. He always took the opportunity to help them when they had EMR questions or just needed a second opinion on a difficult case. He was kind, patient, and empathetic. He understood what they were going through, and he was a phenomenal role model.

And then he died by suicide.

"Yeah, I did," said Ben. "I just saw him a couple of weeks ago at the hospital coffee shop. He seemed happy. He was telling me about his son's second birthday coming up. I am just so shocked."

"I feel so awful for his family," Maya said. "His kids are only four and two. His poor wife. I didn't know he was struggling so badly."

With this news, the suffering of the medical staff at the hospital had become outwardly visible. Ben and Maya knew he wasn't the only one who felt hopeless.

"I walked into the team room the other day, and it was just silent," Ben said. "It's like no one even knows what to say anymore. We're all just sad. His obituary was still sitting on the table, too."

"Sad and frustrated," said Maya. "Two different hospitalists snapped at me last week. Everyone is just angry. Probably because we are all just expected to keep doing our jobs like nothing happened. Did you get the email the other day? What was the line? 'If needed, staff members are encouraged to seek psychological support.' And then they linked to some resources... Like I have time for that anyway," said Maya curtly.

It's true, the hospital had tried to offer support, but it fell way short. Individuals could get counseling, but there was no hospital-wide discussion or effort to understand how the hospital system itself could have contributed to a situation like this and how it might prevent it in the future.

"And then, they followed up that email with the one about the new quality metrics they're rolling out and the launch of the new program on clinical documentation improvement," said Maya. "Back to business as usual. We're all supposed to just move on."

From deep shock, the hospitalists in the group did try to slowly move on. They continued to focus on their patients. They put their heads down and worked. They touched base with each other and made sure their colleagues were doing okay. But the situation continued to weigh heavily in their hearts and minds.

How Ben and Maya chose to react to the death of their peer, however, led their lives in very different directions.

THE PATHS DIVERGE

"I've been thinking, Ben, and I'm just not sure I can keep this up for the next thirty years," Maya said on a handoff call the next month. "One week on, one week off just isn't appealing to me anymore. I'm burned out. I have tried meditation, exercising every day, and mindfulness, but those just don't seem to be enough for me."

"I'm burned out, too," Ben said. "But what else are we supposed to do? At the end of the day, I still need to make money. I mean, look at our parents. My parents worked nearly every day of their lives when I was growing up. Same with your dad."

"Yeah, but medicine was a lot different back then," Maya countered. "Doctors had a lot more control and there weren't as many administrative hoops. Doctors didn't spend their days clicking boxes on the EMR, you know? They didn't have the sheer amount of labs to follow up on. Things just weren't that complex. And they had a lot more autonomy and control over how they delivered care. They actually got to focus on their patients. This just doesn't feel sustainable anymore. Maybe I need to look for another job? Maybe I should be a Starbucks barista. Did you know they get great healthcare?"

"Don't even go there, Maya," Ben said.

"I'm not even kidding," Maya responded. "What else are we supposed to do?"

"You've put a lot of time and effort into being a doctor," Ben said. "How could you consider anything else? At the very least you need to keep going until you pay back your student loans. Maybe you can save aggressively and retire when you're fifty-five instead of sixty-five? As for me, I'm just going to keep doing what I've been doing. I have no choice. I have bills to pay. And not only that, but my family struggled so I could go to medical school. I can't let them down."

"Yeah, I understand," said Maya glumly. "I'll talk to you next week."

A NEW OUTLOOK

Maya hung up the phone from her handoff call with Ben and looked out her living room window. Behind her, Jay looked at his wife, knowing there was more going through her head than she was letting on.

"Hey, are you okay?" he asked.

"I don't want to do this anymore, Jay," said Maya, turning toward him. "I've been reflecting on how I want to lead my life, if I want to keep working full-time like this—one week on, one week off—for the next thirty years. And the answer is, no, I don't want to keep doing this. I mean, I love my patients. I find immense joy when I help someone transition to end of life, or recover from pneumonia, or learn what's going on in their body and feel a sense of control over the future. I want to keep being a doctor, just not in the way that I've been doing it."

"I feel you," Jay responded kindly. He confessed he had been feeling the daily grind, too.

"I hate that our work lives feel dictated by the whims of the clinic administrators," he shared. "I feel like as soon as I have one thing handled, they add another. I don't want to keep up this hectic pace, feeling like I'm running from room to room, behind, seeing patients. I don't feel like I have the time to really help them when I only have fifteen-minute visits! I want to have thirty-minute visits. I want to focus on my patients and be present for them. I want to be that doctor who has the time to care and make things better. I mean, I love what I do, I just want to do it *and* also have a life outside of medicine, too. And I want to spend more time with you."

As it stood, Maya worked every other weekend and Jay worked five days in the clinic during the week. They only saw each other two weekends per month. This was not sustainable now, let alone when they would have kids. They faced a future of limited time spent together as a couple *and* as a family if something didn't change.

"I don't want to do what everyone else around me is doing. I don't want to live the life my parents did," Maya shared.

"What do you mean?" Jay asked. "Your parents were pretty successful, no?"

"Yes, they were, but I want to be there for our future kids more than my dad was for me, you know? I want to be the mom who is there for their birthday parties and soccer games, or whatever it is that they're into."

She paused, looking down at the ground. After a moment, she looked back up at Jay. "But moreso, Jay, I want us to dream again, to imagine anything is possible for our lives. I want to live life on our terms."

"That sounds great, Maya. Count me in. But how are we going to do that?"

"I don't know," Maya admitted. "I don't know how to get there, but that's what I want. You'd think someone would have figured it out by now, right? And we wouldn't be in the situation of watching colleagues who are running at this pace for thirty-plus years."

She didn't want to continue grinding away, but she knew they would need more money to free themselves and live the life she had started to dream about.

"We could cut back to half-time," Jay threw out. "I know doctors who work half-time and they seem much happier. They even have time to make it to their kids' activities and spend time with their spouses." He paused for a second. "But we don't have the money to do that with how we're living now, unless we drastically change our lifestyle."

"Or stop paying down our student loans," Maya retorted.

"Or work until we are one hundred!" Jay joked.

"Yeah, no thanks. I don't want to wait until we're of retirement age to enjoy our life," Maya said. "I mean, yes, my dad worked and worked so he could have a comfortable retirement. But now he and my mom don't travel much because of his dementia. It's like they deferred their whole lives to get to retirement age, and once they got there, they never even had a chance to enjoy it. I don't want that to be us."

"Is there a way we could work 0.75 FTE in the next couple of years or just retire earlier?" Jay asked. "Like, what if we retired in ten or fifteen years, rather than in thirty? What would that look like? What could get us there?"

"That's a great question," said Maya. "How would we even start to figure that out?"

They both thought for a moment.

"Why don't we try looking at our finances and figuring out where we are first?" Jay offered. "Maybe if we know the reality of where we are currently, it'll give us ideas about what is even possible."

"That's a good idea. Let's sit down and go through everything—maybe at some fancy coffee shop that'll set us back the cost of a shift or something?" Maya joked. "There has to be a way," she added more seriously.

They looked at their calendars and found a Saturday they both had off, two weeks from now.

"There. We have a date," Maya said, looking excitedly at Jay as she blocked off that time on both of their calendars.

"It's time to purposefully plan our future and figure out how to live life on our terms."

CHAPTER 4

A LOOK AT FINANCES

*"Risk comes from **not** knowing what you're doing."*

—WARREN BUFFETT

Maya and Jay walked into Starbucks on their first day off together, two Saturday mornings later.

"Double tall soy latte, please," said Maya, ordering her usual. "No foam."

Jay followed, "Grande cappuccino, please."

They settled into a table in the corner by a window and opened a laptop. It contained spreadsheets with their financial information. Over the prior two weeks, both Maya and Jay had gathered data from their bank accounts, credit card statements, loans, and current retirement accounts to calculate their net worth. It was a solid starting point. Since they now knew where they stood, they could start figuring out where they wanted to go.

"We aren't as bad off as I thought we would be," said Jay. "I mean, our net worth is negative, but not as bad as I imagined."

"I was pleasantly surprised, too, even though it's in the red," Maya said. "Here's the thing, though: it's going to be amazing to look back in five years and see where we started and where we end up. I read somewhere that self-confidence comes from doing hard things. When we take this negative net worth and turn it into something positive, it's going to be gratifying to know we put the work into doing it."

"Couldn't agree more," nodded Jay.

"So, looking forward, where do we want to go? I think we should focus on figuring out how the both of us can cut back to part-time in five to ten years. I'd also like to completely retire from medicine ten years early at age fifty-five, as opposed to when we're sixty-five. What are your thoughts on that, love?"

"That certainly sounds amazing, but I have no idea how we're going to do that," Jay said with a concerned look on his face. "But, it does seem reasonable to start with a goal and then work backward."

"Okay, so let's decide on one unified goal, then. The goal is for us to both retire at age fifty-five, agreed?"

"Agreed," Jay said, extending his hand across the table for an official handshake. Maya took his hand and gave it a shake. "Okay then. Let's take a closer look at where we're at."

Despite the fact that Jay and Maya were maximizing their 401(k)s, it was not lost on them that those funds were inaccessible until they were sixty-five without incurring significant fees. This made retirement at age fifty-five using those funds impossible, unless they did something dramatically different than what they had been taught by their parents and financial advisors.

"My parents just maximized Dad's 401(k)," Maya said. "I never saw them do anything else. I think they have enough money to cover retirement, but I guess I don't know for sure."

"I don't think my parents even did that," Jay said. "My guess is they're planning to live off of Social Security and the equity they have in their house for retirement. But we don't want to do what our parents did, so let's figure out an alternative. The most obvious answer to get us to retirement quicker is to save more—and maybe to put some of that money in an investment in bonds or something safe like that on the side."

"Let's see," Maya said, checking her education loans tab on the computer. "We are on track to pay off our student loans in two years. Once we do that, we could direct that chunk of money to savings and put it into an investment account."

"So, if we put away $5,000 per month for the next...fifteen years...," Jay paused as he plugged numbers into a spreadsheet, "and put it into bonds, we would probably have enough to retire on as long as we saw an 8 percent return per year. But bonds and CDs don't get us close to that. We'd have to put it into the stock market into index funds or something like that. I mean, it wouldn't be a huge amount of money, but we could at the very least reach our goal of stopping working at age fifty-five."

"If we significantly cut back on spending, lived off my salary alone, and managed to save $10,000 a month, it looks like we could get there in twelve-and-a-half years at an 8 percent return per year though!" Maya said sarcastically with a pained look on her face.

Jay stared back at her blankly. "Well, that's one possibility. Although that's still twelve years from now and requires cutting spending way back for a long, long time. And I still don't understand how we get that 8 percent return per year without taking on significant risk. I mean, what if the stock market crashes ten years in? That'll potentially add years to our timeline. I'm not sure there's anything we can do about that though."

"Plus we aren't taking into account having kids and the costs that come with that," Maya added. "I can't imagine we could add in daycare, diapers, and other baby expenses and not dip into that $10,000 in savings a month."

She continued: "Another option would be to make more money now so we can save more toward retirement. We could put that extra money in those index funds. Let's see, if I picked up an extra four shifts at the hospital, that would make a difference in how soon we get there—except it would bump us into a higher tax bracket. An extra four shifts would actually be equivalent to only working an extra two and a half after taxes." She paused and pursed her lips. "Hmm. That wouldn't work for me. I can't see myself picking up four extra shifts for the next twelve to fifteen years. I'm pretty exhausted as it is."

"Yeah, that's not ideal," Jay said. "Meanwhile, I'm already maxed out working full-time at the clinic. There aren't moonlighting shifts I can pick up there, and I don't want to work weekends in urgent care—though, I guess I could work the weekends you're working. But that would mean that I only have four days off a month."

"That's not ideal, either," Maya said. "Picking up more shifts and working harder is not the answer. I see what working more shifts has done to Ben. It's literally destroying his health—poor guy. We *cannot* do that. We need to think about other options."

She paused for a moment, thinking. "Could you start your own practice? That might free up some time."

"I don't want to be involved in the business side of medicine, though," said Jay. "I love my patients. And our clinic is way better than most. If I could just work a little bit less, I'd be really happy there."

Maya and Jay considered the other doctor side gigs each of them could take on to earn more money. They could do chart reviews on the weekends. They could try multilevel marketing. Jay had a friend who was an OB/GYN selling skin care. She seemed to be doing well. They could also do something like start a blog, buy a franchise, or buy a business like an IV bar or a medi-spa.

"The problem with all of these," said Maya, "is they're just another job and many of them are higher risk. They'll take a lot of time, and we don't know if they'll even be successful. That's the opposite of what we want to do right now."

Their discussion moved back to exploring ways to cut back on their lifestyle now to reach their goal of retiring faster.

SPENDING, SAVING, AND INVESTING

Maya and Jay weren't huge spenders as it was. They still drove the used cars they'd bought during medical school. They didn't own many toys or designer purses or clothing. They didn't belong to a country club or even eat out that frequently. Even so, they looked at other opportunities to decrease their spending.

"We could move to a less expensive home," suggested Maya. They currently rented a house for $3,600 a month while they continued their search for a house to purchase.

"That's true," agreed Jay. "If we downsized to an apartment, we would probably pay at least $1,000 per month less in rent."

Maya nodded. "That's $12,000 a year right there." It seemed like a good move.

"We could put off buying a house and put our down payment money into stocks like Apple or Tesla," Jay proposed. "If those companies do well, it could be worth a lot more in five years."

"But it could also be worth a whole lot less. We don't have any control. It's a complete crapshoot, and I am not willing to take that type of uncontrolled risk." She paused. "You know, I read about this group of people online doing what they're calling the FIRE movement—Financially Independent, Retire Early."

"Oh yeah, I heard about a guy with a money mustache who

blogs about it!" Maya laughed. Jay was referring to the blog "mrmoneymustache.com." "The method sounds relevant to our goals. How do they do it?"

"Basically, you put money away in extra stock market accounts— accounts you can access, unlike retirement accounts," Maya explained. "The goal is to get to a point where you save enough that you can retire early and live off the money in those accounts."

"Yeah, we started talking about that possibility earlier, but it sounds like it'd take a long time to get there."

Maya pulled up a website on her computer and stared at it intensely. "It sounds like those doing this rely on the stock market and follow what they call the 4 percent rule—they pull 4 percent out each year to live on because that is how much your stocks are assumed to reliably grow in a year."

"Hmm. Stocks are *assumed* to grow 4 percent annually, but it's not a guarantee," Jay said. "That's what I was talking about before—what if the market crashes right before you need your money? You're totally dependent on the stock market and whether it goes up or down."

"It does seem a bit risky," Maya said. "You're just hoping the market doesn't drop, or that the ebbs and flows still balance out to 4 percent growth." If they were making a pro-con list for the FIRE method, that was a definite con.

"So generally speaking, how much are people who have FIREd living off of?" Jay asked.

"Well, it looks as though many of them live pretty frugally to make it work. Take this guy for example," Maya said, pointing at the screen. "He was a computer programmer who retired when he was thirty-five, but he lives on $30,000 a year now—which I admit, is entirely too low for me. You'd need something like $4 million saved up to have $150,000 a year to live on."

"This FIRE method *could* get us to early retirement," Jay said, pausing for a moment. "But do we really want to live on, say, $60,000 to $80,000 a year for the rest of our lives? I mean, what if something happens, like one of us gets cancer or one of our kids has extra needs? Don't we want to have the flexibility to pivot in life with financial abundance if we need to?"

"Yeah, that's true," Maya said. "I don't want to ever be in a situation where we are barely getting by and then have something happen. We'd then be really stuck."

It was another con to add to the list.

"Plus, I don't think we could even do this until we paid off our student loans," Jay said. While they were working hard to pay their debt down, they still owed about $50,000 each. They currently paid $5,000 per month toward student loans.

"True. We already know we need to work for at least two more years just to pay those off," Maya added. "And only then, could we start the FIRE method."

"And for $80,000 a year, we'd need $2 million saved," Jay said. "If we diverted our student loan payments to this, it could still take us almost fifteen years. We might be able to do it faster if the stock market goes up more than 8 percent, but if it goes down, it could take even longer. If the stock market drops by 50 percent, we'd effectively have to earn a 100-percent return just to get back to where we were. Just think—if we put in $100,000 and the market drops by $50,000, we have to double our money to get back to neutral."

"Ugh, that's horrible. It makes me uncomfortable relying solely on the stock market. What if there's a downturn? We have no control over that, and our money could be locked in there for years and years. Plus, we could be in a situation where we retire for a couple years and then become suddenly financially strapped, forcing us to go back to work. At that point, we would have lost our skills!"

"Oh gosh, you're right!" Jay exclaimed. "That would suck."

The list of cons was growing. The FIRE method didn't seem to suit Jay and Maya's needs.

"Saving and investing in the stock market with index funds seems like more of a really long-term play—and one where we have *no* control," Maya said. "Unless we decide to invest in individual stocks, but that's so risky—because we'd be doing it relatively blindly."

"What are the other choices for investing besides stocks anyway? There have to be other options!" Just as Jay asked this question, his phone buzzed with a new text message. It was their realtor. He read it and sighed, looking up at Maya.

"Our offer wasn't accepted. We were outbid again. The house

went to another buyer." It was their tenth rejection over the last year.

"Well, maybe this is a blessing in disguise," said Maya. She was feeling fed up with all the rejected offers, and she didn't have an answer to the investment question Jay had just asked. "I think we need time to research finances to see what else is out there, and to see if there's even a way to retire early or work less sooner rather than later."

She looked at Jay and smiled. "I'm confident we *will* find a way."

CHAPTER 5

THE EPIPHANY

"They go to their financial planners or accountants or stockbrokers and buy a balanced portfolio. Most have lots of cash in CDs, low-yield bonds, mutual funds that can be traded within a mutual-fund family, and a few individual stocks. It is a safe and sensible portfolio. But it is not a winning portfolio. It is a portfolio of someone playing not to lose."

—ROBERT KIYOSAKI

Back in their respective roles after their first financial discussion together, the daily grind had begun to wear on Maya and Jay. They needed a vacation.

Two weeks in New Zealand sounded like heaven.

They had booked their one and only travel that year months ahead of time and looked forward to some rest and relaxation, some quality time together, and some new scenery. To honor their adventurous spirits, they had rented an RV and planned to drive around the country, camping at trailheads to beat the hiking crowds. When Maya and Jay arrived in New Zealand, they realized that what they had heard from others was spot on—the country had some of the most epic hikes and views in the world.

The food was out of this world, too. Maya and Jay ate delicious farm-fresh meals, which was the standard fare there. They marveled over the orange egg yolks that floated high above the whites and the depth of flavors found in the grass-fed meats, butter, and cheeses. When they didn't eat at restaurants, they cooked basic meals in their RV with fresh produce they bought at farmers markets.

One day during their visit, they stopped by a cherry orchard to pick their own cherries. The dark ruby cherries mesmerized Maya, and she took her time finding and gently picking the darkest cherries she could find. The owner of the orchard had told them the darker the color, the sweeter the cherry, and Maya wholeheartedly agreed. Maya and Jay walked away with 1.5 kilos of cherries after spending a few hours enjoying the orchard—which they munched on for days afterward.

Without access to electricity, the evenings were spent reading. It was a much slower pace, and they relished the time they had together not glued to their cell phones or computers.

Despite the slower pace, Maya was still on a mission to figure out how to get them to financial freedom sooner rather than later. She held tightly to the belief that she would find a way. Although she had heard many doctors repeat the platitude "Doctors aren't good with money," she refused to believe that.

Why wouldn't doctors be excellent with their money? she thought. *We're critical thinkers. We're smart and can learn new things. It's just a matter of putting in the time to learn the skills. I know I can do a great job of managing our money.*

With that in mind, Maya dove into the book *Rich Dad Poor Dad* by Robert Kiyosaki. It was a recommended read by two respected doctors and financial bloggers she had recently started following, Peter Kim of Passive Income MD and Bonnie Koo of WealthyMom MD. She figured the book could help give her a foundation as she went more in depth researching financial independence.

Within the first few chapters, Maya was so enlivened with what she was reading that she had to share it with Jay. In the flashlight glow of their tiny RV, they began reading the words, line by line, to each other. With every few sentences, their eyes lit up with excitement about the ideas the book was introducing.

"Employees trade time for money," said Maya, pacing back and forth in the camper as she restated concepts from the book to Jay. "So right now, we're employees. If we work a certain amount of time at our jobs, we get paid for that time. It's a 1:1 equation of trading time for money."

"Self-employed people do the same thing," Maya continued. "The amount of time spent working equates to the money they make. But business owners and investors, now that's different. Their income does not depend on how much time they spend actively working because, in the case of business owners, their employees are doing work that makes them money. They have leverage. And in the case of investors, the investment makes them money. So, their money works for them, rather than trading their time. They make money in their sleep!"

CASHFLOW QUADRANT

E	B
E	**B**
Employee	**Business Owner**
Amount of active work determines income	Income does not depend on active work
Time = $$$	Employees = $$$$$
S	**I**
Self-Employed	**Investor**
Amount of active work determines income	Income does not depend on active work
Time = $$$	Money = $$$$$

Adapted from *Rich Dad Poor Dad*
by Robert Kiyosaki

The concept was simple, but at the same time, mind-blowing.

"So this is what our parents did their whole lives," said Jay, tapping his index finger on the employees section of the quadrant, "and we're on the same track, trading our time for money as lifetime employees. There's no way we could retire in ten to fifteen years on this track, no matter how much we've built up in retirement funds. We're just on track to become comfortable retirees late in life. That's why we couldn't figure out a faster way to get there when we crunched our numbers."

"We need to become investors or business owners with employees, so our efforts are multiplied beyond what we can do ourselves," nodded Maya.

"Right. If we're investors or business owners, then we wouldn't have to trade time for money. So...should we look to buy a business that is on sale? Is that what that means?" asked Jay, looking confused.

"Yeah, I guess. But what business would make sense for us? A restaurant? A medi-spa, maybe?" asked Maya. "I don't know much about owning a business."

"Yeah, me neither. It sounds like it would still take up time to learn and get those skills."

"Well, how about real estate?" Maya asked. "Robert Kiyosaki invests in real estate, and it's clearly worked for him. Plus, we've loved looking at properties together during our *incredibly* extended house hunt. We already know the basics of buying a house. I think it would be fun!"

"Yeah, but wouldn't real estate investing also eat away at our time?" Jay countered. "We're trying to do something to free up our time, not put more on our plate. I don't see how real estate investing would fall under the investor quadrant, either. We'd still be trading time for money, no?"

"Well, it looks like when you invest in real estate like Robert Kiyosaki does, you're technically in two quadrants: business owner and investor. In the book, he talked about how he walked through different neighborhoods looking for properties for sale. When he found them, he'd meet with the owners and negotiate great deals on buying them. He then rented them out for a rate that made him money each month. So those properties made him money without him having to do much, besides buying the property and keeping it maintained. That's what made him an investor, because he would make money while he slept from rent and the properties gaining value. And it sounds like he's made quite a lot of money doing it."

"Okay, I get that it would put him in the investor quadrant, but I don't understand the business owner part," Jay admitted.

"My understanding is that you're a business owner because you own the property that's making you money," Maya said. "And you have 'employees' (*she used her fingers to make the quotation mark gesture*) who consist of other people running the property—property managers, contractors, landscapers, and so on. They're technically not on payroll or anything. Instead, they're your leverage, and they're working to make you money."

"Oh, I get it now," Jay said. "So with each new property, it's like buying a new business. And you're investing in something that will bring in money, because you can basically outsource a lot of the work to other people."

"Yes!" Maya exclaimed. "But you're also an investor in that your properties make money each month in rent and become worth more over time independent of the hours you spend on them. So your money is also making money for you without you having to actively expend a 1:1 ratio of your time and energy. Your time and effort become multiplied since your investment is making you money with minimal effort."

Maya, it turns out, already had some experience with investment real estate. When she worked on Wall Street, she had purchased a few pieces of raw land, holding onto them for six months or so, and then selling them at higher prices. She sometimes turned quite a bit of profit with a sale, but that didn't generate any monthly income for her like Robert Kiyosaki did with his rental properties. And she had to sell the land at a loss when there was a downturn and it lost value. She wasn't eager to do that again. But now, reading this book, she realized what was previously missing—cashflow. She had to sell her properties during the recession because she couldn't afford to keep them precisely because they weren't making her money each month. She and Jay needed to buy things that paid them money every month instead of costing them money to support.

"You know, Jay, somewhere I read that 'raw land eats three meals a day' and now I finally get it," Maya said. "Back when I was on Wall Street, I was buying pieces of land in Florida and then flipping them a few months later to buyers who were willing to pay more. Everything at the time went up and up and up in price—it was exhilarating. But then, when everything came crashing down, I was stuck paying mortgages and taxes and maintenance for years until I sold for a loss. Did you know I had to actually come to the table with cash to sell the properties?! It was terrible."

"What I didn't see then was that these pieces of land were liabilities," she continued. "Like Robert Kiyosaki says, they weren't making me money each month. They were costing me money to support. That wasn't so bad when I could just hold onto them for a couple of months and then sell at a higher price to make money. But I definitely felt it when I couldn't sell them because they had lost so much value—and then I had to pay out each month to support them. So I had to work harder each month just to pay all my mortgages. I'll never do that again. No more betting on the market going up to make money. I want my properties to make *me* money."

"Totally agree," said Jay. "We need cashflow."

"Yes, cashflow is what can replace our monthly incomes."

RISK MANAGEMENT

As they continued to read *Rich Dad Poor Dad*, Jay and Maya started to see how everyday people could build enough cashflow to replace their incomes from their day jobs. They also soon realized that what they were currently doing—relying on just their incomes alone—was what was truly risky. They only had their physician incomes to support them. What would happen if they had a crisis and couldn't work? They had a false sense of safety.

"Well, at least we have two sources of income between both of us," Jay pointed out, since they both worked full-time. "But if going through the COVID pandemic has taught us anything, it's that things can change in an instant. Remember how long my clinic was shut down? And how all those surgeries were canceled and the specialists were furloughed for months? My office was closed for just a couple of weeks, so we didn't take a huge financial hit. But that could always happen again and last longer. We need to be better prepared, personally. We need to have multiple sources of income to weather any financial bumps along the road. Our physician incomes are not enough."

"Also, what would we do if one of us got sick?" Maya asked. Maya had a colleague whose wife had been diagnosed with breast cancer the year before. She saw the pressure he was under juggling a full-time job, plus covering a nanny for the couple's two little kids and supporting his wife through treatments. As the sole breadwinner, he couldn't even afford to take FMLA time to be home. He looked exhausted all the time.

"I have seen the stress in his eyes," Maya said. "I don't want that if something happens to either of us or our family members."

"Or what if one of our jobs becomes unpalatable?" Jay added with eyes wide. While he loved the family medicine clinic he worked at, he knew many other clinics had shifts in new management recently, completely changing the work environment for doctors. Many of them wanted to leave and work elsewhere, but they couldn't find jobs that paid competitively. "I don't want to be stuck working somewhere I hate because I have no other options."

The couple had a small rainy-day fund of about $15,000 (in addition to the down payment set aside for their primary residence), but still, the way they were headed now, if something happened to one of their jobs, the other person would have no choice but to continue to work full-time just to pay for the new house they were considering purchasing.

Suddenly, the idea of trading time for money with no other sources of income didn't feel so secure.

In fact, relying on the traditional financial advice they'd received from advisors and modeling the conventional path to retirement paved by their parents was riskier than they had realized—and maybe, it was even *holding them back*.

"What we're doing right now is putting us in a position of what *Rich Dad Poor Dad* calls 'playing not to lose,'" Maya said. "It's ensuring that when we're sixty-five, we'll be comfortable. That's what everyone around us is aiming for. They're just stocking up for when they're sixty-five. But what about before that? What about being comfortable when we're younger? What about enjoying our journey along the way? What about generating true wealth—generational wealth? Reading this makes me think there's a way to go beyond playing not to lose."

She took a pause.

"I want to play to win."

ASSETS AND LIABILITIES

Maya and Jay kept reading. The chapter in *Rich Dad Poor Dad* on assets and liabilities was even more eye-opening for Maya and Jay, and it reaffirmed that they needed to change course and figure out a way to generate monthly cashflow.

"According to this," Maya said, tapping her finger on the open page, "assets put money in your pocket at the end of the month after you've paid all your costs. So, for example, let's look at a rental property you own. After you've paid all the costs of maintenance, property taxes, everything else, and you still have money in your pocket, that's an asset. The property makes the money that pays for the costs, and you make money on top of that."

"Liabilities take money out of your pocket each month," continued Maya. "This book says a primary residence is a liability because you have to pay to support it. It's like owning a car. What many consider to be 'investments' are actually liabilities since they don't put money into their pockets. For it to be an asset, it has to generate regular cashflow."

"We haven't bought any assets then," said Jay. "We only have liabilities. Even the index funds in our retirement accounts, though they're not liabilities, aren't paying us any money each month. They are either growing or losing value depending on the stock market. Hopefully, they'll be assets down the road when we sell them, but ultimately, we have no control of what they do. The stock market is going to do what it is going to do. If we had stocks that regularly paid us dividends, though, we'd have assets because they'd be paying us regularly."

"If we want to replace our incomes, we need assets," said Maya. "And this new home we've been planning on buying isn't going to be an asset, it'll be a liability. It'll cost us each month to support it, pay our mortgage, property taxes, insurance, and then to take care of maintenance."

"Right," said Jay. "It's a liability month to month. But most people buy a primary residence thinking it'll gain value. They're thinking it's going to appreciate in value over time."

"But there's no guarantee of appreciation," countered Maya. "When you bet on appreciation to make money, you're gambling. You have no control of what is going to happen with the market. And, if you have a liability, you're paying out to support it each month. I know what that feels like from my experience with buying raw land—and I don't want to do it again."

"Plus," added Jay, "If we took that same money we'd put into a down payment on a house and put it into an investment property that actually made us money each month, we'd be using that money to make us money rather than costing us to support a house."

They looked at each other.

"We should rethink buying a home," Maya said.

"Maybe we should," nodded Jay in agreement. "We need to drastically change what we're doing if we want to be financially independent in ten to fifteen years. We can't just keep doing what we've been doing and expect a different result."

"No, we certainly can't. I think it was Einstein who said insanity is doing the same thing over and over again and expecting a different result, right?" teased Maya.

"Yep," laughed Jay. "And I'm not insane!"

"You're not?" Maya joked, nudging Jay playfully.

In Maya's head, fifteen years didn't seem like such a stretch for financial independence now. She thought back to the 4 percent return they could *potentially* expect in the stock market, and how they would need $2 million saved just to live on $80,000/year using the FIRE method. To her delight, Maya now realized there was another potential avenue of investing that would require saving less capital and allow them to reach their goals more quickly.

After a pause, she looked at Jay and asked, "Do you think we could reach our goals sooner than we initially planned?"

"What do you mean?" Jay asked, raising an eyebrow questioningly.

"Well, fifteen years seems like a long time," she responded. "Reading this makes me think we could do it even faster. It also makes me think that medicine wouldn't need to be all or nothing. Maybe we wouldn't have to retire completely if we didn't want to, but we could replace our income so we could choose how much we practice and where we practice. Maybe we could even do it in less than ten years."

"You mean by investing in real estate?" Jay answered.

"Exactly. This book gives a lot of examples of buying properties, renting them out, and using that form of cashflow to support a lifestyle. We're not talking about buying huge apartment complexes. I mean, Kiyosaki bought single-family homes and small multifamily properties. I think we can do that."

"My only remaining concern is being a landlord," said Jay. "Don't landlords get called in the middle of the night for issues all the time?"

"I don't know," answered Maya truthfully. "Though if I'm being honest, getting called at night every once in a while may be worth it to me if that gets us to financial freedom in less than ten years."

"Yeah, I don't know," Jay said, rubbing his chin. "I think we need to learn some more before we really jump on the real estate bandwagon."

REAL ESTATE INVESTORS EMERGE

In the days that followed, Maya and Jay added more books to their Kindle on real estate investing, including some that offered examples of real people who had successfully built cashflowing portfolios.

Reading real-life examples of real estate millionaires showed Maya and Jay that there were many paths to wealth through owning rental properties—and that many people had journeyed before them. They also saw that many successful real estate investors had even lacked the resources that they had as professionals. At least as doctors, they had fairly high, stable incomes and no difficulty getting loans.

Reading others' stories, they also discovered that there was a wide range in how people built their portfolios. They could build a portfolio in any way that was comfortable for them. They could invest in just single-family homes, small multifamily, larger buildings, or even commercial spaces or self-storage or medical office buildings. They could self-manage or have property managers do the majority of the day-to-day work and pay them a fee. They could use leverage by buying with a mortgage or could choose to pay cash and not have debt. There were many examples of regular people who had built up significant portfolios following a wide range of paths by adhering to simple principles and continuing to work day jobs the entire time.

This was possible for them, too.

Maya and Jay also learned they could make money on their future properties not only from the monthly cashflow, but also as their renters paid down their mortgages—and if their properties gained value over time from market appreciation (though they weren't going to bet on that!). They could see the path to buying multiple properties, each bringing in additional cashflow that, eventually, would produce a steady stream of income. With enough properties bringing in cashflow, that would mean they could replace both their clinical incomes. They also started to learn about the various tax advantages associated with owning rental properties, which would help them grow their portfolio faster than they even initially imagined.

As they read book after book, they started to gain the confidence that they, too, could be real estate investors.

"I think we can do this," Maya said excitedly. Jay agreed. They had officially settled on real estate investing being the avenue through which they would achieve their goal of financial independence.

"So, what do you think our goal should be?" Maya asked. "How much cashflow through investment properties do we need to live our lives the way we want?" Maya made about $300,000/year as a hospitalist. Jay made almost $150,000/year as a family medicine doctor. "Do you want to shoot for $100,000 as our goal?"

"Hmm," Jay thought for a second, lightly rubbing his index finger over his bottom lip. "How about we try to replace my salary?"

"Oh yeah? Well, once we pay off our student loans and if we downsized our lives, $150,000 in cashflow would make it so we would never have to work again if we really needed to. We can live on that."

"We could definitely live on that. And we're not even considering the tax benefits. I mean, the way real estate investing is set up to be largely tax-free, it seems like making $150,000 in real estate cashflow is really like making more like $200,000."

"Replacing your salary it is!" Maya declared. They had established their starting goal: to generate $150,000/year through investing in rental properties. "What's our timeline then? I'm thinking we should aim to do it in five years. What do you think, Jay?"

"Is that realistic, do you think? I mean, could we really actually expect to do that? Isn't it too short? Maybe we should say ten years?"

"Honestly, I don't care what's realistic." said Maya with determination in her eyes. "Instead, let's ask ourselves: What do we *really* want? I strongly believe that's where we should start. Then we'll figure out the actions to get us there. We're capable of doing anything."

"That's not how people usually do it, Maya." replied Jay. "Usually people decide on what they think is reasonable, what can realistically be done, and then they aim to do that."

"That may be true, but we don't have to do what everyone else does all the time, do we?" questioned Maya. "Besides, we've seen lots of examples in these books of people who didn't have many of the advantages we have. So we know it's possible—it's just a question of how fast.

"Plus," she continued, "Don't you think that aiming big will make us stretch to figure out how to make it happen? If we just aim small because it seems doable, I think we limit ourselves from tapping into what we're capable of doing—and cutting off the opportunity to have a phenomenal outcome because we thought small from the beginning. I want more for us than that!"

"Okay okay! I can get behind aiming high," laughed Jay, shaking his head in admiration of his wife's fire and drive. "But don't you think that could be a lot of work? Are we really ready for that?"

"It probably will require a lot of focus, energy, and determination. But if we don't do something, we'd just continue following along the same path. If we do this, though, we could be living the lives of our dreams in less than five years! We could be working half-time. We could be volunteering on medical missions. We could have most or even all our weekends with our kids. Don't you think it's worth putting in some effort to have the lives we truly want?"

Jay thought for a moment. "I do," he finally said, with commitment in his voice. "Compared to doing what we are doing now for the next thirty years, I know it will be worth it. We are doing this for our future and our kids' futures."

"This is absolutely the right path," said Maya. "Five years to $150,000 in cashflow it is."

And with that, their goal was set.

TAX SAVINGS WITH REAL ESTATE

Maya and Jay decided to focus on gathering additional needed skills to become real estate investors for the remainder of their New Zealand trip. To do this, Maya started reading everything she could in order to deeply understand the tax advantages of real estate. She knew if she could figure out a way to reduce their taxes using some of the real estate tax advantages vaguely alluded to in their earlier readings, they'd be able to take those tax savings and buy more real estate investments sooner, getting them to financial independence even faster than they had initially planned.

Through her research, Maya started to see that, at baseline, real estate was naturally a tax-advantaged investment method thanks to the ability to write off losses, including ones that weren't even real losses but rather "paper losses," like depreciation.

Maya excitedly shared her new knowledge with her husband.

"Jay!" she exclaimed. "Come here, come here! I need to talk to you about depreciation!"

"Deprec...eh, what?" Jay asked. "Please slow down, love, and tell me exactly what you're talking about."

"Well," Maya said. "In the government's eyes, every investment property loses value each year. Over the course of 27.5 years, for example, the structure of the building that you buy as an investment property goes from whatever value you bought it at to zero."

"Why does that matter?"

"Well, every year, you can write off 1/27th-and-a-half of the value of the building's structure as a loss on your taxes. So it's an expense on your taxes. Taking this 1/27th-and-a-half yearly loss of the building's structural value is called straight-line depreciation. When you take straight-line depreciation every year, you can write this off as a passive loss on your taxes. And losses shelter gains on your taxes. In fact, these passive losses usually shelter a substantial chunk of what the property is bringing in as rental income, meaning that most—if not all—of your cashflow from your rental property is tax free because of depreciation. That's why people say that making $100,000 in cashflow in real estate is really like making closer to $150,000—because you often aren't paying taxes on the income you bring in. This is unlike if you work at your job and get W-2 income. The income you make by being a physician is taxed at a normal rate because you usually can't find ways to shelter it besides putting it in your 401(k), for example."

Maya continued: "Sometimes you even have extra leftover passive losses from your real estate that you can use to shelter any other passive income you might have. So, for example, if we owned part of your clinic and got distributions from our shares, we could shelter that passive income with any leftover extra passive losses from our real estate investment portfolio."

"Oh wow. That's incredible," Jay said. "But wait. Let's play this out for a second." He pulled out his calculator. "For a property we purchase for $250,000, we divide that by 27.5 and end up with $9,000 a year in a loss we can write off in taxes? Is that right?"

"Well, no, actually," said Maya. "It's the building structure's *value*. Only the building structure can be depreciated, not the land. So in the $250,000 property you referred to, if the land was worth $50,000, for example, you'd depreciate the building value of $200,000 over 27.5 years, so your losses taken on your taxes would be around $7,300 a year, not $9,000. But what's really crazy is that these are what they call 'phantom' or paper losses, meaning they aren't real losses. I mean, they are real losses on your taxes but not losses in real life. No money comes out of your pocket. In fact, your property might actually be increasing in value each year—so you're actually gaining in net worth, but the government still counts the investment as decreasing in value. Isn't that amazing?"

"That's pretty wild, actually," Jay admitted. "So, let's say we made $10,000 a year of profit on that $250,000 property example.

We could shelter $7,300 of that profit with our 'phantom' loss from straight-line depreciation. Then, according to the books we've read, we could write off repairs, mortgage interest, our home office, our phone and internet bills, and our business meals and travel expenses, right? That could add up to more than $10,000, which would mean we'd have excess losses to further shelter other sources of passive income?"

LEARN MORE

For a deeper dive into depreciation, check out semiretiredmd. com/life-depreciation.

"Yep!" said Maya. "But remember, we'd still be making money despite showing a loss on our taxes! Because depreciation is a phantom loss, not a real loss. So we would still make monthly cashflow but show a negative on our taxes at the end of the year. Plus, if you do improvements to your property, like you rehab the kitchen and then charge more rent per month, you can write off the costs of that rehab as a loss on your taxes as passive losses too. So it's effectively like the government is paying for you to do part of your rehab—and that rehab creates more cashflow and increases the value of the property, all of which you keep!"

"So by using the phantom/paper losses created by straight-line depreciation, we can shelter our real estate cashflow with phantom losses and not pay income tax on our real estate income?" Jay asked, wanting to ensure he fully understood. "If we did that, and didn't pay much, if any, taxes on real estate income, but continued to pay income tax on our clinical income, we'd be reducing our overall tax rate. Like, if we get $300,000 in real estate cashflow and $300,000 in doctor W-2 income, we could cut our tax rate in half using depreciation from our investment properties—is that right?"

"You got it!" Maya said excitedly.

"What if we created more 'phantom' losses with depreciation and doing rehabs and improvements on our properties than we had in real estate, but we didn't have any sources of passive income to shelter?" Jay asked. "What would happen to those extra losses? Would they shelter our W-2 income or lower our tax rate even more?"

"Well, if I understand it correctly, W-2 income is 'non-passive income'—or, as some call it, active income—and passive losses from real estate cannot shelter active income from your job. But those passive losses will continue to carry forward until they get used up someday when we sell the property and have passive gains so we don't pay as much in taxes on the money we've made. Another way we could use the passive losses would be to have a passive investment, such as a franchise or medical office or a real estate syndication or something that makes us monthly passive income, then our passive losses would shelter that passive income."

And that was not all. Maya found another way to reap tax savings by sheltering their active W-2 income from taxes using their future rental properties.

If either Maya or Jay spent the majority of their working time in real estate and a significant amount of time "materially participating" in the operations of their personal investment properties, they could shelter some, if not all, of their clinical income. They could potentially not pay *any* income taxes by using paper real estate losses. This was possible as long as one of them achieved a tax status called real estate professional status (REPS). As married high-earning doctors, one of them meeting criteria for REPS could make a huge difference in their financial picture and get them to their five-year goal even faster.

"The person who claims real estate professional status needs to spend greater than 50 percent of their working time in real estate and at least 750 hours total in the calendar year," Maya explained to her husband. "One of us could meet criteria by spending more than 500 hours on the day-to-day operations of our portfolio of investment properties, and then 250-plus hours on other real estate–related activities. This would transform our losses from real estate from passive to non-passive (active) losses. And then we could use those active losses to shelter active income—like our clinical income—from taxes. Suddenly, if we created enough losses with depreciation and rehabs, we wouldn't have to pay income taxes. Can you imagine what that would do to the growth of our net worth, Jay?" exclaimed Maya.

"Well, that sounds worth it," Jay said. "Should one of us get the status?"

"We'd need to see if it would make sense for us to cut back with the taxes we'd save. I currently work sixteen days a month at twelve hours/day," said Maya, calculating. "So I'm working 2,300 hours/year. If I came down to half-time, I'd need to do

1,151 hours in real estate to meet the criteria of more than 50 percent of my working time being spent on real estate. On top of that, I currently make $300,000 per year. So we'd reduce our income by $150,000 if I went half-time."

"Meanwhile, I'm working thirty-two hours a week, so that's about 1,500 hours/year," said Jay. "I'd only need 769 hours of real estate to get the status if I went half-time in the clinic. I could definitely cut to part-time. It will reduce my salary by half, so we'd take a cut of $75,000, but if we sheltered that and your entire salary from taxes, we'd probably get close to the difference in tax savings per year. We'd essentially be neutral.

"But," he continued, "we'd be making money beyond just the tax savings. We'd be bringing in cashflow, the renters would be paying down our mortgage, we'd have the potential for market appreciation..." Jay ticked things off his fingers. "And I know we'd be able to grow our real estate portfolio faster because I'd do a better job if I was spending half my time focused on it. Plus my schedule would be way more flexible. We'd actually have more time together on your weeks off if I only worked two-and-a-half days a week."

"Good points, love," Maya said. "I think it makes sense for us to try to have you do it, then. Since we're done with this year, we'd have to commit to buying enough properties next year that you'd have enough work to take up more than 770 of your hours. So, we'd probably have to buy several investment properties and do a couple of rehabs to make sure you can get all the hours. Are you ready to jump in, both feet first?"

"I'm committed to our future," answered Jay firmly. "And I'll do anything to get us there faster. This is a clear way to get us there much faster—so yes!" He took his two thumbs and pointed them at his chest. "You're looking at a brand-new real estate professional. I'm going to get the hours next year, no matter what! It's a must."

LEARN MORE

To learn more about real estate professional status (REPS), visit: semiretiredmd.com/life-reps.

MINDSET SHIFT

The idea that Jay would work more time in real estate than in medicine was a change that excited both of them in a way that shifted their whole mindset—they weren't just doctors anymore. They were serious *real estate investors*, and they weren't going to just buy a property or two, they were going to build an empire.

Maya knew they needed to lock in their decision to cement this identity change, and the best way to do that was to take action—now. She began by sending an email to the real estate agent who was helping them look for a primary residence.

"There's been a change of plans," Maya wrote. "We no longer want to purchase a primary residence. We are real estate investors now, and we'd like your help with finding invest-ment properties."

"Wow," replied the agent a couple of hours later. "That's cer-tainly a shift! It's outside what I usually do, but, yes, of course, I'm ready to help."

Jay spent the last few days of their New Zealand vacation scouring Redfin for local Seattle properties for sale whenever he had internet access. "I'm going to email our agent and ask him to put in an offer on this property," Jay said to Maya the day before they flew home. "I'll ask him to go in low and see what happens."

"You don't think we should look at the place first?" Maya asked.

"I read that a lot of real estate investors don't see properties until they get them under contract," Jay responded. "So I think we need to just put out offers to take the first step, you know? I don't want to get stuck in analysis paralysis. I want to push through the fear and make things happen as soon as possible."

And so it began. They knew where they wanted to go—$150,000 in yearly cashflow in less than five years. And they had identified the vehicle to get there—investing in income-producing rental properties.

Yes, it would require time, effort, and focus. But together, they'd accept the challenges that were bound to come their way and grow together as they tackled them.

If they could make it through med school, they could do this, too.

CHAPTER 6

A CHANGE IN PLANS

"Courage is not the absence of fear. It's the ability to triumph over it. A brave man is not one that does not feel afraid. It's he who conquers that fear."

—NELSON MANDELA

Home from vacation, Maya and Jay sat down to take a second look at their finances and figure out how to use what they had to jump-start their real estate investing portfolio.

To start, they agreed that going forward, putting money toward cashflowing properties was the priority. But this new way of thinking meant making some serious changes to how they chose to spend their money.

They had already settled on the decision to not buy a primary residence and, instead, continue to rent for the foreseeable future. They also shelved the idea of getting a new car, which was something they'd discussed the last couple of months. "I think if we get into a situation where we have to buy a new car because one of our current ones dies, we should lease," said Maya.

"Agreed," said Jay. "That way, we don't have a chunk of money depreciating in a liability when it could be used in a property that would generate cash instead."

"And, if we have to lease something, we lease a used vehicle," said Maya. Jay nodded.

It was a little funny how quickly their view of things and plans had changed so dramatically in such a short period of time because they aligned on a shared goal. "Would I rather have a new car that depreciates and costs us money to maintain or an income-producing rental property that gets us one step closer to living life on *our* terms?" Jay asked.

They both knew the answer.

REASSESSING SPENDING HABITS

Up until this point, Maya and Jay hadn't really been diligent about creating a budget each month. They had been focused on setting aside their allotted savings for their student loans and their future home. But they hadn't spent any time examining the little everyday expenses that were adding up.

They decided to change that.

Jay and Maya gathered their respective credit card bills from that calendar year. They each highlighted what they deemed as unnecessary expenses. They also reviewed their shared bank account and the checks they had written.

"We definitely have a Starbucks problem," Jay said. "Between the two of us, we're spending ten to fifteen dollars a day, on average, on coffee and food when we're working. That adds up to several thousand dollars each year. We can definitely cut back there."

"I think we can cut back on clothing purchases, too," Jay continued. "Sorry, love, that means fewer visits to Nordstrom." Maya smiled. It was a sacrifice worth making. They decided to also decrease the overall amount they spent buying items like hiking and camping gear.

"I don't want to cut traveling out, though," Maya said. Jay agreed. They would continue giving themselves a budget of $7,000 per year for trips. They also decided to keep their monthly professional cleaning service for their home. They felt the time savings translated into more time they could spend on real estate investing.

They also discussed the potential for geographic arbitrage—that is, moving to an area with a lower cost of living and higher pay—to speed up their journey. They could move to a more rural location—say, to Texas for example—where they would have larger salaries and still not have to pay state income taxes.

"I don't want our kids growing up without their grandparents around, though," said Jay. Maya's parents lived in the Seattle area, and they looked forward to the close bond their future children would build with them. In the end, they decided relocating was a sacrifice they were unwilling to make.

"Not every decision should be made only based on finances," reflected Maya.

"That's true," agreed Jay. "We need to determine the sacrifices we are willing to make but also know we don't have to sacrifice *everything*. Not every decision needs to be economically based—and that's okay. We need to make decisions that are right for us."

TAKING ANOTHER LOOK AT 401(K)S

After settling on a new spending budget, Maya and Jay moved to discussing other ways to access the funds needed to start their portfolio. This included rethinking their 401(k)s.

"We could liquidate our 401(k)s," Jay threw out. Maya and Jay lived in Washington State, one of several states with no income tax, so they wouldn't have to pay that if they liquidated their accounts.

"Yeah, but if we do that, we'd have to pay a 10 percent penalty and significantly higher federal income taxes since the lump sum we'd get from our retirement accounts would be considered income," Maya said. "Plus, we can't liquidate our 401(k)s from our current jobs. We'd have to quit to access that money. So really, we could only liquidate our retirement accounts from your residency years and my time on Wall Street."

"Hmm." Jay thought for a second. "The money we have in our current work retirement accounts is really trapped. It's almost like it's in *money jail*."

"It *is* in money jail," agreed Maya. "You know, I always thought of our retirement accounts as safety blankets. And they really are that. They're safety blankets that give us a feeling of security for when we're old. But by putting money in them, we also lock up that money from being used now, to grow our wealth for our benefit in the near term, so we can have the lives we want now instead of waiting until we're sixty-five. Maybe we should reduce our 401(k) contributions going forward instead? That would allow us to have more money we can put into real estate investing now instead of deferring our wealth to the distant future. How does that feel to you, Jay?

"As it currently stands, we are contributing the maximum amount possible to each of our retirement accounts, plus the $6,000/year matches our employers provide," Jay said. "If we stop maximizing our contributions, it could provide more money to invest in real estate—that extra money could potentially buy us an additional property per year."

He raised his eyebrows at that possibility, but it somehow felt wrong—and against every piece of financial advice he had ever heard.

"If we both continue working as full-time doctors, lowering our 401(k) contributions would result in a tax rate hike, though," Maya said as she plugged numbers into her calculator. "We would pay an additional $12,000 in taxes each year between the two of us working full-time if we didn't maximize our 401(k)s, and we'd give up our employer matches. But you're not going to work full-time. You're going part-time at the clinic so you can get real estate professional status. So the actual loss would be a bit less."

"And with earning real estate professional status, if we bought enough properties, we could create enough paper losses to completely shelter our clinical incomes. This means we wouldn't pay anything in taxes. Plus we could potentially even shelter the money we withdraw from our 401(k)s on top of sheltering our incomes, if we used our 401(k) money as down payments on additional properties," Jay said. "This would mean that we continue to have our effective tax rate at zero even with liquidating our 401(k)s. All we would pay would be the 10 percent penalty." They looked at each other.

"This could be a way to build our portfolio more quickly," Maya said. "Though the 10 percent penalty would be painful to pay."

"Yes, it would." replied Jay. "But, if we bought something that was cashflowing, we could potentially make up that fee in a year. The bigger question for me is whether we should really mess with our 401(k)s? Every piece of financial advice we have ever gotten says to max out our 401(k)s, to build up a large nest egg now so we can retire later. That's what everyone does and says to do. Are we really considering *not* doing that?"

He looked worried.

"I don't know, Maya," Jay continued. "What if we fail at this real estate investing? We wouldn't have the cashflow we thought we'd have, we'd pay the 10 percent penalty, *and* we'd have less to retire on later. Are we destroying our future by reducing our 401(k) contributions?"

"It would definitely go against the norm," admitted Maya. "And, yeah, not doing what everyone else does feels almost foolish. Not doing what we've been told to do from every single financial advisor out there is scary."

"Plus," Jay interjected, "what have we always heard? *Doctors aren't good with money. Leave it to the professionals.* What if we aren't good with money? Should we really go against the dogma of financial experts everywhere?"

"I hear what you're saying, but do you think that could just be something financial advisors say because they are making money off of investing doctors' investment accounts? I mean, how many financial advisors tell their clients to go out and buy real estate investments? I don't think most financial advisors know much about owning rental properties. Their expertise is the stock market. They make money off of every dollar their clients put into the stock market. So really, when you think about it, financial advisors don't have an incentive to advise their clients to put their money anywhere outside of the stock market.

"Yeah, that's true," Jay agreed. "Most financial advisors do make money from the fees they charge managing people's stock and retirement portfolios. It wouldn't make financial sense for them to advise people to invest in another vehicle. Maybe this is something we're just going to have to trust ourselves on, even though it's a little nerve racking."

"I have an idea," said Maya. "Let's flip the notion that doctors are bad at investing on its head and come up with reasons why doctors are actually great at managing money. For one, we have critical thinking skills and the ability to rapidly learn and implement new skills. I refuse to believe we can't learn to do this!"

She looked down for a moment, and then looked up to meet Jay's eyes. "Our entire lives, we've done everything that has been expected of us—pre-med, MCAT, med school, residency, fellowship...*save aggressively in our 401(k)s*. We did everything we were taught. We followed all the steps to what we were told would be a certain future as doctors. Yes, not saving for retirement like we've been advised to do veers from that path of certainty—it goes against everything we've ever known. But everything we've ever known was to play it safe, just get by, and maintain the status quo. With this real estate investing journey, aren't we aiming for more?"

Jay paused. "Yes, we are," he conceded.

"I don't want the status quo. I want to play to win."

"Okay, what if we don't go quite as far as liquidating our 401(k) accounts, but instead reduce our contributions to the level where we just get the match and see how that goes?" Jay suggested. "That would be a bit more cautious, but it would still allow us to grow our portfolio more quickly. We can always increase our contributions again if we decide cutting back wasn't the right choice, and we aren't getting the results we expected from our investment portfolio. But if we do generate the cashflow we expect, we may never even *need* our 401(k)s."

"Yes!" replied Maya passionately. "We're going to be so wealthy later that we won't even need our retirement accounts to support ourselves. We're going to live off our real estate cashflow instead."

Jay smiled at his wife's determination. He had to agree. It made sense to put every dollar toward building their real estate portfolio, despite the fear they both felt making that decision.

Jay and Maya were aligned in the decision to cut back their 401(k) contributions to just what they needed to get the full amount of their employer's match. They also agreed to revisit the decision in six months to ensure they still felt it was the right one.

REALLOCATING SAVINGS

After looking at spending habits and 401(k)s, Jay and Maya turned their attention to their savings and how to best use it as they began investing in income-producing properties.

"We have $150,000 saved up that we initially wanted to use as a down payment for a home," Jay said, reviewing their bank account summaries. "I think we should use that as our down payment to buy investment properties, and then put all of our savings toward investing in real estate from now on."

"It's a little scary to use all of our savings from now on, isn't it?" Maya asked. "Maybe we hold a small nest egg but use the majority of our savings?"

That seemed fair, they agreed, and relieved some of the stress of knowing they were living without savings. Still, they'd need more money to build the portfolio they envisioned.

"What about our student loans?" Maya said.

Jay looked at her like she was half crazy. "What about them?"

"Well, we could stop paying extra toward them and just pay the minimum," she suggested. "The interest rate on those is only 3 percent and we could use that extra money for investing."

Just like the 401(k) decision, this felt extremely risky and for-eign to both Jay and Maya.

"So, we would essentially be keeping our loan debt longer while also taking on more debt by financing our investment prop-erties?" Jay said apprehensively. "We'd be getting more loans on top of our student loans and not paying off those loans. That feels...wrong."

"It does go against everything we've ever been told, which is to get rid of debt as soon as possible," Maya nodded in agreement. "But what if we actually create more cashflow this way and then use that to pay off our student loans? I read somewhere that Robert Kiyosaki bought cashflowing properties and then used the cashflow to buy liabilities like fancy cars, instead of buying the fancy cars first. This would be like that. We buy investment properties that make us money that we then use to pay off our student loans as we see fit."

They both fell silent. Were they really considering doing this?

"Think about what wealthy people do," Maya reasoned. "Remember what the books we read said about the truly wealthy? Wealthy people use good debt to their advantage to build their wealth. That's what we'd be doing, right? Intelli-gently using debt to grow our wealth—not just racking up credit card bills and using high-interest loans to buy liabilities. We're buying assets—assets that will make us money."

"That is true," Jay said. "It just seems like we'd be taking on more debt, which is the opposite of what we've been trained to do."

"But, we've been trained to do what's safe. Which makes sense for most people who just want to do the safest thing possible and get by—people who don't want to play outside the sandbox."

"Yeah, we're committed to doing something bigger," Jay continued her thought. "We *are* playing outside of the sandbox. We don't want to just get by. And that means taking some risks."

"And there are potential payoffs to the risks. We are risk mitigating by getting properties that cashflow. That's a little different than just putting our money into stocks or appreciation plays and crossing our fingers that they go up. What we're planning to do is buy real assets that make us money each month, which seems a lot less risky than hoping for something we have no control over."

Jay nodded his head in agreement. They both thought for a moment, trying to make a final decision.

"I think we may need to muster some courage during this real estate journey," Maya said. "Doing something even when we're afraid—that's courage."

"We'll definitely need it," Jay said. He then smiled. "I do believe we have the courage to do this. And the skills. I mean think about it, as doctors, we've been trained to reach goals, make educated decisions, and look at the upsides and downsides in all situations. Our medical backgrounds really qualify us for success here."

"That's right," said Maya, going in for a much-needed hug. "I know there will be times we are scared or worry we aren't making the right choice, but instead of letting that stop us, we need to make sure we move forward. And hey—the reality is that we are going to make the wrong decisions sometimes, but we will learn from them. This isn't going to be all smooth sailing, but we are going to grow, and we are only going to get better over time."

"Well said, my love," nodded Jay. "Someday we'll look back at this and remember the uncertainty, the challenges, and the times we persisted in spite of it all, and it's going to make our victory that much sweeter."

"One hundred percent," Maya said, winking at her husband.

After much debate—and mustering of courage to do something they'd been taught their whole life *not* to—Jay and Maya decided to only pay the minimums on their student loans going forward. The savings this would add to their real estate investment fund, plus the $15,000 per year they estimated they'd gain by lowering their 401(k) contributions, and the additional $20,000 per year their new budget would save them, should be enough for a down payment on an additional property purchase each year.

It felt exciting—and scary—but most of all, this dream they had of achieving financial freedom while they were still young enough to enjoy it was starting to feel real. They were inching closer to putting their new plan into action.

FOCUS ON CASHFLOW

Having agreed on a new budget and way to handle their current and future finances, Maya and Jay's next focus was how to project cashflow. How much cashflow should they expect each property they purchased to make each year?

They started by researching and reading online real estate blogs and websites. It was through this research that they discovered the concept of cash-on-cash return.

"Cash-on-cash return is the amount of cash you get back on what you invest into a property," explained Maya, reading from one of the websites she had up on her screen. "So, for example, if we put $100,000 into a property purchase—that includes down payment, closing costs, and any money we spend rehabbing the property—and we make $10,000 in cashflow per year after paying all expenses, that's a 10 percent cash-on-cash return."

"Ah, interesting," said Jay, looking on. "Your cashflow and cash-on-cash return numbers don't take into account renters paying down your mortgage, tax savings, market appreciation, or something called forced appreciation, though. So in the end, cashflow is just a small part of the return that you get as an investor. But I can see how important it is to have cashflow. It says here your cashflow is not only the money that can replace your income, but it's also 'your buffer' in case there's a downturn or major repair, or you have a prolonged vacancy. But what's forced appreciation?"

"I don't know, exactly," admitted Maya. "Let me look it up." Maya pulled up another website. "It says here that forced appreciation is the increase in value of a property that an investor can create when he or she increases its income or decreases its expenses. Since investment properties are bought and sold by investors, their value is based on how much cashflow they produce for the next owner. So, when you increase the amount of money your property makes after you buy it—like a small business—then you increase its value to the person who buys it from you down the road."

"Ah, gotcha." Jay finished scanning the article. "Wow. We already knew that cashflow is the key to replacing our income and freeing us to work in medicine on our terms, but I didn't realize how many other ways you also make money investing in real estate. I also didn't understand how that can all add up to grow your net worth substantially in a fairly short amount of time. Let me see..." he used his finger to count all the ways: "(1) Cashflow (2) Renters paying down your mortgage (3) Tax savings (4) Immediate appreciation—when you buy the property at a discount (5) Forced appreciation, and (6) Market appreciation. That's six different ways you make money on a rental property."

He looked at Maya. "No wonder people make so much wealth in real estate compared to the stock market! When you add all that plus the ability to use leverage, which you definitely don't get buying stocks, it's pretty crazy how much of a return you can get. I mean it can easily be 20, 30, 40 percent and even higher! Maybe we should set a cashflow *and* a net worth goal for ourselves, huh, Maya?"

"Yeah, maybe. But for right now, let's focus on what we want as our standard cash-on-cash return for the properties we buy. This blog advises thinking about a baseline for cash-on-cash return *before* investing in properties. It says you can use a cash-on-cash calculator to see how much return a property can yield before you even put in an offer. So if you have a general sense of what you're looking for with cash-on-cash return, you can run the numbers on properties before you even put in offers to see if the properties will get close to your cash-on-cash return." The blog linked to a calculator, so she clicked on it.

LEARN MORE

To learn more about forced appreciation, visit semiretiredmd. com/life-appreciation.

"What do you think our cash-on-cash return criterion should be?" she asked, as she started to plug numbers into the calculator for a property they were considering putting in an offer on.

"I've seen people aiming for a 10 percent cash-on-cash return for long-term rental buildings in other places," Jay said. "Why don't we make that our rough goal for now, but aim for higher once we get our feet wet?"

"If we invest our money in two long-term rental properties with 10 percent cash-on-cash return, that'd get us $20,000 in cash-flow this first year. That seems doable," Maya said reflectively.

"Hmm," said Jay as he furrowed his brow, "$20,000 doesn't seem like very much. When you compare that to our current salaries, it's not much money."

"I see what you're saying, but those first two properties would just be the start," Maya replied. "Sure, they won't make us rich, but if we learn how to invest in real estate, we can keep doing it again and again. It'll just be 'rinse and repeat' afterward. I bet we'll get much better at it as we learn more, too. Once we have four or five properties, even if they're each only bringing in $10,000 or $15,000 a year, it'll start feeling much more significant."

"Is all that effort to learn real estate investing worth it, though, just for $20,000 in cashflow in one year?" Jay countered.

"The way I see it is, the first couple properties won't set us free, but the skills we learn *will*. Learning how to make money this way could change our lives. Once we have the knowledge of how to successfully invest in real estate, we can keep building our portfolio until we get to financial freedom. It won't happen overnight, and that's okay. It's going to take time to achieve mastery. It's going to take time to get enough properties to set us free. But, either way, I'm confident we'll get there much faster than we would just investing in the stock market or our 401(k)s."

"That's true," said Jay, reassessing his apprehensions. "And once we have the skills to make money through real estate, that's something no one can ever take away from us. It's not like we're just handing our money over to a financial advisor and never retaining any knowledge or confidence about how to make money. It will be *us* doing it."

"Exactly. I truly believe these first properties are just the start of something bigger. Plus, remember all the other ways we make money in real estate you just mentioned? Maybe we'll only have $20,000 in cashflow, but we'll also be making money in lots of other ways. Our renters will be paying down our mortgages, we'll be harvesting those tax savings, we'll add value to our properties by making them make more money—that's forced appreciation—and maybe we'll even experience some market appreciation. So, in the end, we'll be making much more than just the cashflow," Maya finished, feeling confident.

"True," Jay said. "I also believe that anything we put our mind to, we can achieve. Maybe we shouldn't limit ourselves to what seems 'doable' and strive for even more cashflow."

"That's the spirit, love! What about $50,000 in cashflow as a goal for this year?" Maya suggested.

"I don't know exactly how we're going to do that, but let's go for it!" Jay said optimistically. "At the very least, aiming high will make us push and think in new ways to get there. If we don't make $50,000 exactly, that'll be okay."

The conversation had provided just the reminder they needed that they were challenging themselves to do something *big*. That meant aiming high when setting their goals and cultivating the mindset that would allow them to achieve them or even get close to achieving them, even despite the initial fear and uncertainty of how they were going to do it.

LEARN MORE

Read why investing in one rental property may not make you rich, but it will, in fact, set you free: semiretiredmd.com/life-oneproperty.

With a rough cash-on-cash criterion established, Jay and Maya then asked themselves: What would they do with the cash from their properties when it started coming in? And what would they do with the tax savings that they got each year as a result of investing in real estate?

"Well, I think we have two options for our real estate earnings and tax benefits," Maya laid out. "We could spend the cashflow and tax refund checks to live, but $50,000 a year in cashflow and whatever tax savings we collect next year won't come close to replacing our incomes."

"Or, we could funnel the cash and tax savings back into buying more properties," said Jay. "That would allow us to build our portfolio a lot quicker, especially when you consider compounding. If we had $50,000 in cashflow and even just $50,000 in tax savings, those will add up quickly."

"It's just simple compounding," Maya agreed. "The faster we can build our portfolio, the sooner we can start completely replacing our monthly incomes. When we add our cashflow and tax savings back to what we're already planning saving up from our salaries, we should be able to buy multiple properties a year." They smiled at each other, giddy at the thought of amassing a portfolio of properties so quickly.

"So that's our plan," Maya confirmed. "We're going to recycle every single dollar in cashflow and tax savings back into buying more properties."

Jay and Maya proceeded to crunch some numbers of other properties in the cash-on-cash calculator when their phones lit up. It was a new email from their realtor. Maya opened it. "Oh. We didn't get the property. Someone else bid over the offer price."

"You know," Jay said, "I know this was our first offer, but perhaps we should consider working with someone else? Our current realtor is a nice guy, but does he have the knowledge to help us build an investment portfolio? Are we going to be as successful as we could be if we continue to use him as our agent going forward?"

"I do like him," nodded Maya, "but he doesn't seem to have the experience we need to help us lock up deals. I'm not even sure he's a useful thought-partner when we run the numbers, either. He has admitted finding investment properties isn't something he normally does. We've spent a lot of our time educating him on what we've picked up from books and blogs—and we're just starting this journey! I mean, he's nice and all, but what would a *great* agent who really understood real estate investing do for us?"

"That's a good question. Maybe we need someone who has investment property experience and knowledge. Someone who works primarily with investors," Jay suggested.

"There are agents that only work with investors?"

"From what I've read, there are investor-friendly agents who work mostly helping investors buy rental properties. They understand the numbers, know the neighborhoods well, and even have connections to solid team members you need, like property managers and contractors."

"Well, I do think we could get our first purchase quicker if we had an investor-focused agent!" Maya threw out. "And I personally would prefer someone who can teach us and guide us instead of the other way around."

LEARN MORE

Your real estate agent is critical to your success as an investor. Learn the difference between a residential and an investor real estate agent by visiting: semiretiredmd.com/life-agents.

Jay nodded. "And I'm sure it'd positively impact our long-term growth, too, having someone who knows the ins and outs of purchasing investment properties. Maybe we can even find someone who owns rentals themselves, so they truly understand what it's like to be an owner."

"Yeah, I'm tired of trying to explain things like cash-on-cash return to our current agent. But...I feel a little bad letting him go, especially since he's been so eager to help."

"There's another way to look at this, Maya." said Jay. "Maybe his time would be better spent serving other clients who are looking for primary residences, which is what he's good at. Maybe we'd actually be doing him a favor by moving on with an investor agent."

"Ohhh...yeah...that makes sense. I don't want to waste his time, either." Maya took a deep breath. "Okay. I know the best thing for everyone involved is to go our separate ways. I'll call him tomorrow and let him know."

PUSHBACK

Despite their first offer being rejected and making the decision to cut ties with the real estate agent, Maya went in for her hospitalist shift the next day feeling enlivened by her and Jay's new goals and dreams.

Strangely, planning their financial growth through this real estate adventure had breathed some new spirit and purpose into Maya's career as a doctor. Her previous burnout felt a bit less burdensome, because she was starting to feel like staying at her job would be a choice soon, not a requirement. She enjoyed planning her future from a space of empowerment and possibility. She was no longer a helpless victim of her circumstances. She already felt a little more free.

She walked into the doctor's lounge to grab a bottle of water before seeing her first patient when she ran into her colleague, Olivia. Olivia was a fellow hospitalist, and over the years of working together, the two doctors had become friendly.

"Hi, Olivia!" Maya said cheerfully.

"Hey, Maya. You seem like you're in a good mood. What's going on?"

Excitedly, Maya began telling Olivia all about her and Jay's new plan to invest in real estate and the actions they had already taken to make it a reality.

Olivia furrowed her eyebrows and gave Maya a questioning look as she listened.

"But...you're a doctor," Olivia said with confusion. "How will you have time for this?"

"Well, this is important to me, so I'll find the time," Maya responded. "Jay and I have chosen to make this a priority."

"But why in the world would you add something *more* to your plate with everything already going on here?" Olivia asked. "Don't you already feel overwhelmed most days?" She knew how burned out many of her colleagues were, including Maya. She also deeply felt the challenges of balancing a hectic full-time hospitalist job plus a family, since she had two young children of her own. How could Maya think it was a good idea to add more to her responsibilities?

"Sure, it may be adding more to my plate, but with our end goal in mind, it will be worth it," Maya explained. "This is a priority for me because it means freedom for the rest of my life. It will give me the ability to work in medicine on my terms, to be there for my family, and to not sacrifice myself or my happiness anymore. Heck—I could even cut down to part-time here at the hospital if I wanted!"

Olivia looked at Maya with disapproval in her eyes.

"You'd only practice part-time?" questioned Olivia. "It seems like a waste of time and money to have gone through medical school to do that. Why would you throw away all your training just to work part-time?"

"I wouldn't be throwing it away...it's just that...," Maya stuttered.

"I think you owe it to society and your patients to work full-time, don't you?" Oliva continued.

"Well, sure, but don't you think—" Maya started to say.

"I mean, everyone knows the *really* good doctors practice medicine full-time," Olivia continued. "It's what we're meant to do! If you're distracted by real estate, how can your patients know you're focused on them?"

"Well that's the thing. I'll be able to focus on them more—from a place of—"

"I don't know, Maya. Are you sure this is the right decision?"

Maya didn't know what to say. She *thought* she was sure about investing in real estate. She and Jay had done so much planning and had discussed all of this over and over again. But she had to admit—there was an inkling of doubt forming in the back of her mind after hearing Olivia's points.

"Well, I have to get to my first discharge," Maya said. "You know the new policy about getting people out by noon! It was nice catching up." She tried to force out a smile and walked away to start her rounds.

Later that evening, after a long and grueling shift, Maya got back to her car to go home. Her neck ached and her head pounded. She had been so busy she hadn't had a bite to eat or even taken a sip of water all day—probably a good thing since she also wouldn't have had time for more than one bathroom break anyway! But now, her body was reminding her of its neglect. She was hungry, dehydrated, and thoroughly exhausted.

Yet, all she could think about was what Olivia had said.

Good doctors practice medicine full-time.

You owe it to patients and society to work full-time.

Don't you have enough on your plate?

The words echoed through her brain. She knew Jay would say just the right thing to make her feel better, but maybe Olivia was right? Were she and Jay crazy to be doing this?

She needed another opinion. And who better to call when making a huge decision about her future in medicine than—Dad.

Maya's mom answered the phone.

"Oh, hi honey! We were just talking about you! Dad and I were trying to find a time to come up to visit you and Jay. I know with your schedules it's nearly impossible to find time to see you both together, but maybe we could squeeze in a dinner next month?"

"Hi Mom, yeah, I'm sure we can find time. Let me talk to Jay when I get home, and we'll see what we can do," Maya said tiredly, dismissing her mom's request. "Hey, is Dad there? I have something I want to ask him about."

Maya's father got on the line after a brief pause. Maya told him about her and Jay's realization on their trip to New Zealand, their real estate investing plans and her goal to eventually be able to cut back to part-time as a doctor. She asked what he thought.

The pause on the other end of the line felt like eternity.

"Maya, you're a doctor, not a real estate investor," her dad said sternly. "Why would you throw away your career after all those years of training? And lower yourself to do something like real estate, when you're a physician—an MD Maya! There's a certain status in that title."

Maya drew a deep breath in. She'd expected some pushback from her father. He was a very proud, retired MD. He had dedicated his life to practicing medicine. But she didn't expect him to get this upset.

"Dad, practicing medicine is different now than when you did it," she tried to explain. "It's draining the life out of me. We don't have autonomy anymore. We can't do what is best for our patients. I literally feel like I push paper around all day. Real estate could allow me the freedom to practice medicine on my own terms—to work at a job where I don't have to see as many patients every day. To actually do what I think is right for my patients. I might even have a chance to go on those medical mission trips you used to go on to India, if I can work part-time or get a job that actually has vacation days!"

"You think you're unhappy now. You know what will really make you unhappy? Losing it all. What if you lose everything you've built in this real estate venture?" her dad asked. "Real estate is risky, Maya. You could find yourself broke, unable to pay your bills because you built up so much debt and bad investments.

"That's exactly what happened to your Uncle Joe," Dad continued. "Remember that? He had no idea what he was doing. He bought all those expensive condos in New York City. Then he couldn't find renters who would pay enough to cover the mortgages. He ended up having to sell his family's house. His kids had to switch schools. It was a mess..."

His words trailed off. There was nothing more to say. Maya's head spun. Was she really making a huge mistake?

She thanked her father for his opinions and told him she'd call back at the end of her inpatient week. She drove the rest of the way home feeling dejected. Perhaps Olivia and her father were right. She was in over her head. What did she know about real estate investing, really?

She walked in the door and broke down in tears, burying her head into Jay's chest. She told him about the reaction from Olivia and then what her father had said.

"Maybe they're right, Jay," Maya cried. "We're doctors. We handle people's illnesses, not houses. I mean, look at us. We're going to invest tens of thousands of dollars into rental properties without any real knowledge. We spent years studying to be doctors, but we're going to just do this on a whim? We could lose everything!"

Her crying was now a sob.

"Plus," Maya said quietly. "I can't stop thinking about what a waste all my medical training would be only to practice medicine part-time or quit altogether now. I mean...I took up a coveted spot in medical school—some poor applicant who would happily work full-time as a doctor didn't get in because I took their spot. And think about the cost to society! Yes, we pay nearly $50,000 in tuition, but you know that's supplemented by society. We have a responsibility as doctors, Jay! A duty!"

She had completely spiraled at this point. "I feel guilty that we aren't upholding our duty as doctors if we don't commit our lives to practicing medicine."

Jay took her hand.

"Maya," he said gently. "Yes, we are doctors who spent years studying and being educated. And no matter what we do, we'll always be doctors. Doctors who care about our patients and who want to do the best for them. But that also means taking care of ourselves, too. And think about why we wanted to do this in the first place—how unhappy we've been, how burned out we've felt, the future we want to build together. There are always going to be naysayers, who see all the reasons we shouldn't step out of the path that everyone else is following."

Maya looked up and gave Jay a half-hearted smile. He gave the best pep talks. And she *did* want this—badly. But everything she was feeling—the worry, the guilt—it was real, and it was becoming a lot to handle.

But Jay continued. "Have you considered that we might be better doctors if we have financial freedom and don't need to practice for money? If work was a choice, don't you think we'd show up differently?"

He had a point, Maya thought. "I *have* seen studies that show that burned-out doctors have worse patient outcomes."

"Yes, me too!" Jay said passionately. "And studies have shown that better financial health is related to less burnout in doctors.[2] Just think, where are we going to be in five or ten years if we keep up this pace? Everyone around us is burned out. It's just a matter of time before we end up like that if we keep doing what we're doing. And then what? We are going to deliver worse patient care and our patients are going to suffer. So if we can achieve financial health through real estate, it's actually gonna help us be better doctors and provide better patient care. And hey—we might even stay in the system as doctors for far longer *because* we did real estate!"

Everything he said made sense. Maya had seen that research on the relationship between financial stress and burnout herself, too. Still, she worried immensely about her lacking real estate investing skills and the potential risks they were taking on by not being educated. She needed to feel more prepared before they could move forward.

"Maya," Jay said softly. "One thing I've noticed these last several weeks is how much happier you've been going into the hos-

---

2   Colin P. West, Tait D. Shanafelt, and Joseph C. Kolars. "Quality of Life, Burnout, Educational Debt, and Medical Knowledge among Internal Medicine Residents," *JAMA* 306, no. 9 (Sept. 7, 2011): 952–60, https://pubmed.ncbi.nlm.nih.gov/21900135.

pital. You've seem less drained. It almost seems like starting to take action in building an investment portfolio has already started to help. Is that what's been going on?"

"Something like that," replied Maya. "Just thinking about a future where I know we'll have control of our lives and where we work and how much we work has me already feeling more free. I've started to see that it's all going to be a choice. And I've also started to think that once it's a choice, I'll have the freedom to push back when I see things I don't think are right. I feel like I might be able to change the system even.

"I also feel more present with my patients right now. It's almost like I'm rediscovering medicine because I feel like I'm taking care of myself a little more." She took a pause. "I even feel closer to you. Working on this project together has meant that we've been spending more time dreaming about our future—and then taking the steps to make it a reality. I can't really describe it, but I just feel more in control of my life and less...hopeless."

"See?" Jay smiled. "I think that means we're heading in the right direction, even if it feels overwhelming at times."

"Thanks, love. I don't want to give up what we're doing," said Maya, gathering herself together. "But I do think we should take a pause on putting in any more offers until we get more knowledge under our belts. I want us to know exactly what we are doing. Then I'll feel more confident that we can actually do this, successfully, and not be putting our future at risk."

DIGGING DEEPER

While Maya appreciated the pause from looking at deals and putting in offers over the next few weeks, she definitely hadn't abandoned her dream of owning rental properties. In fact, she found her mind thinking about it more and more.

What do I need to do to gain the right skills? she thought to herself.

That's when, during one of her off weeks, she tuned in to a podcast and the most fitting guests came on the air: two doctors-turned-real estate investors who had started a business to help other doctors do the same.

She listened to the interview with interest and discovered these two doctors shared a lot of similarities with her and Jay. They had been hospitalists who decided they wanted more out of life. They wanted time with their family and time to travel—they wanted financial freedom and to not solely rely on their medical salaries. They wanted more autonomy and control over their lives.

And they had done exactly what she and Jay were attempting to do: they had built a portfolio made up of both long- and short-term cashflowing rentals that allowed them to work in medicine by choice. At the end of the interview, the doctors mentioned they taught courses to other doctors who wanted to enter—and thrive in—the real estate investing world.

As soon as the episode ended, she called Jay, who was working at the clinic.

"I think taking a real estate investment course taught by these fellow doctors would give us the confidence and skills to move forward," she said.

"They're doctors, too? No way," Jay said.

"It's a seven-week online course. '*Go from knowing nothing to purchasing your first property*,'" Maya said as she read from the website, having looked it up after the podcast ended. "And on top of that, it says here that you will get a community of other doctors, coaches, and mentors investing in real estate to help you along your journey."

"This sounds a little, um, too good to be true?" Jay questioned. "Do you think we should be skeptical about it being so doctor-centric?"

"I did think about that," Maya admitted. "I've heard time and again that if you invest in something and all the other doctors are doing it—run!"

"Exactly," Jay said with a chuckle. "I know we are good at managing money, but there *is* that perception that many doctors are notoriously bad at it. How do we know this isn't a scam?"

"Well, I don't know for sure, but at least this course isn't making any big promises or overarching statements. It says it can take us from knowing nothing to investing in our first property, but we have to put in the time and effort. We are the ones building the skills. It feels like doctors legitimately helping doctors learn how to do it themselves. It's like it was made for us."

"But couldn't we just find everything out there on how to invest in real estate for free?" Jay wondered. "We've already taught ourselves a lot about investment properties in the last three months."

"I'm sure a lot—if not all—of this information is out there for free somewhere...but the time that it'd take us to find exactly what we needed to know, and not get overwhelmed, would set us back months. Wouldn't it be much more valuable to go through a structured program that gets us everything we need to know in just two months? Plus, it sounds like we would have the support of other doctors—just like us! We'd also get some solid help building our real estate team, because they have connections all over the country. I feel like we'd get to the point where we'd acquire the knowledge, a team, *and* confidence faster than if we went at it on our own. We'd probably make less mistakes, too. That seems invaluable when you consider that each deal is hundreds of thousands of dollars. In my eyes, if the course helps us avoid just one mistake, it'll be worth the investment."

"Gosh, well you can't argue with that!" Jay replied. "I love the way you think. You're right. Getting there faster with less risk and surrounded by a community of people who aren't naysayers sounds extremely valuable. Let's do it."

"Thanks, love," said Maya. "I'll get us registered."

CHAPTER 7

MAKING PROGRESS

"Proximity is power."

—TONY ROBBINS

The seven-week experience was worth every penny.

It was no wonder Jay and Maya weren't getting anywhere with their residential realtor. It was no wonder their low-ball offers weren't getting traction. They were making decisions blindly.

While the educational and informative material from the course itself was worthwhile, one of the bigger values that came out of it was the community. The student-cohort of like-minded people they met and collaborated with via a private online group associated with the course gave Maya and Jay the foundational support they needed to move forward as real estate investors.

"You know what the best part of the course was?" Maya asked Jay.

"What?"

"The freakin' community! I can't even describe how valuable it is to connect with others who are where we are, struggling with the same challenges."

"Right? I don't feel so alone on this journey anymore. And most of them are fellow doctors, no less. Plus the coaches and mentors are phenomenal. I can't believe they were in our shoes just a couple of years ago. I have loved learning from all their experiences in different markets across the country."

It was something Maya and Jay didn't expect, and they felt uplifted by the support from the private group they were now a part of. The community provided a welcome reprieve from the criticism they often endured from the naysayers in their lives who just didn't understand what they were doing. The community's support solidified for them that they were on the right path.

"I found it gratifying to hear that other people also struggled with loved ones who don't understand why doctors would pursue real estate investing," Jay said.

"Yeah, same. Their stories, so closely related to our own, made me realize how much of my energy these naysayers were consuming. Don't get me wrong, I love my dad and my colleagues, but they were dragging me down. Their opinions and words made me question myself, which then veered us off track—not to mention how it used up so much of my energy."

"I hated explaining why we were doing what we're doing over and over," Jay added. "It was stressful—and it made me not want to share at all because I didn't want to deal with the questions and negativity. It was refreshing to hear other people had similar stories and then to see their struggles, where they persevered anyway!"

"And not just with the naysayers, but with pretty much everything else. We're all doctors and high-income professionals becoming real estate investors. I feel like the members in the community are helping each other aim higher, setting a high bar for each other."

"I couldn't agree more," Jay said. "You know what my absolute favorite part was?"

"What's that?"

"Seeing what's possible through other people's successes. Some of those course alumni brought in $100,000 in cashflow their first year investing in rental properties—and some did even more. I mean, wow. That could be us in a few years!"

"I love how everyone posts about what they're doing as they're doing it—it's exciting and inspiring," added Maya. "I've learned a lot just from following along with their questions and seeing how the coaches and mentors responded."

The feel of the community was one of genuine support. Sometimes in the hospital and clinic, Maya and Jay had interactions with other physicians that were adversarial and downright unpleasant. But there was none of that here. Everyone cheered each other on and helped each other when they were in tough situations.

"I gotta be honest," Jay said. "I was a little skeptical about a community of doctors helping doctors, but boy, do we understand each other, eh?"

"Ha! I know, right? The level of trust and vulnerability you see from everyone is incredible, too. They're sharing real numbers, real struggles, and real solutions."

"I especially appreciated the honest feedback and candor about how people manage their work loads and family responsibilities while also buying properties. Did you read the post where someone asked how doing all of that was even possible?"

"Yes, I did. It was a solid question, but did you see the answers? No one bullshitted us, which was nice. I appreciated people acknowledging that balancing everything is a challenge, but that they are working on finding leverage by getting help in other areas of their lives. I also liked seeing examples of where community members are finding the time. They're all in it for the long haul and know that it will be worth it in the end, just like us!"

"Not only that, but their words of support and encouragement made such a difference for me, too," Jay said. "They reminded us that we have all been through difficult things before in medical school and in our jobs and life—which is undoubtedly true."

"And that we are smart, driven, and resourceful," Maya added. "Whatever happens, we will figure out a way and keep going."

"If we could get through med school and residency and treat patients with complex diseases, we can definitely master real estate investing. If others can do it, then we can, too."

"Agreed!"

Part of the reason the community was as supportive as it was, Maya and Jay learned, was that everyone agreed to abandon the scarcity mindset and instead embrace one of abundance. This meant believing there was plenty out there for everyone. Just because somebody got a deal under contract didn't mean there were fewer deals for others. An abundance mindset also meant seeing what others were doing as building inspiration—not comparing yourself to them or feeling bad about yourself as a result. It wasn't about one person being better than another—it was about helping each other along the journey.

With that mindset, feelings of jealousy or competition were left by the wayside. Everyone instead focused on contributing to the community, sharing resources, contacts, and knowledge, knowing that doing so wasn't going to set them back and would likely come back to them down the road in even more abundance.

JOIN US!

You're invited! Please join our free public community of Semi-Retired Physicians at semiretiredmd.com/life-fbphys or our Semi-Retired Professionals group at semiretiredmd.com/life-fbprof.

With the support from a like-minded community, Jay and Maya turned their attention to the next steps in the journey: choosing a market, building a team, and finding their first deal.

CHOOSING A MARKET

In addition to the emotional support the community provided, it also offered Jay and Maya the opportunity to connect with members who were investing in the same markets. They could share information and resources, and weigh in on deals to reduce blind spots. Through sharing their real investor journeys publicly via the online group, members benefited from communal wisdom and experience.

Before the course, Maya and Jay had primarily focused their attention on properties in their local Washington area. They assumed the only safe way to invest was to do so close by. They were surprised to see members of their community investing in properties out of their home state—something they hadn't considered even possible.

"Do you see how many people are investing out of their home state?" Jay asked Maya one night over dinner. "They're investing across the country, buying properties they haven't seen in person, and even managing renovations from afar. How nuts is that? We could never do that!"

"Wait, why not?" asked Maya. "If they can do it, why can't we? You don't think we can do the same?"

"Oh gosh, no—the thought of it makes me incredibly nervous," admitted Jay. "What if the contractor steals our money? What if he does bad work? What if we have a bad tenant and have to evict him? What if we buy a bad deal that has foundation issues or something else we didn't see? Then what?"

"I share those concerns, too, but don't you think all of those scenarios could happen locally as well?" Maya countered. "If we have a bad contractor, we'll have to replace him with another one either way. We could have a bad tenant, but I don't plan on going through an eviction process myself whether the property is local or not. An inspector could miss a foundation issue even if we were personally at the inspection ourselves. I certainly wouldn't know how to identify a foundation issue, would you?"

Jay thought for a moment. "No, I wouldn't."

"How often do you even see us going to our local properties?" Maya asked. "When we have renters in place, do you think we'll be going over there every week to just drive by the outside of the building? I think, as new investors, we would get some security and certainty by having a property locally, but whether that's based in reality, I'm not so sure. And, I'm worried we are limiting ourselves by only looking locally."

"This isn't a particularly landlord-friendly state...and the cost per unit is definitely higher than other places," Jay nodded, hearing what Maya was saying.

"Exactly. It might be easier to find killer cashflowing properties at a cheaper price elsewhere. And, we don't have diversification across our portfolio if we just invest in one area. That's important to me—and I see us someday having properties in multiple cities and states. If we are going to do it someday, why not learn to do it now?"

"Everything is so new, though. Investing out of state makes me uncomfortable. We don't even know what we're doing."

"Not yet! But we will learn. I mean, listen, Jay, things are going to happen along the way. Maybe a contractor is going to steal some of our money. Maybe we are going to miss a foundation issue. Making mistakes is going to be part of the journey. It doesn't mean we're failures. It doesn't mean we give up."

"I know, I understand," said Jay. "It can just be tough to accept that mistakes could happen when it comes to investing our money. I just always want to make sure we're doing the right thing."

"I hear you, but I do think we need to accept that, sometimes, we are not going to make the right decision, and that's okay. We're going to learn from our mistakes and get better. Remember, that's part of why we are in this course and community—to help minimize our mistakes. But we shouldn't expect to be perfect, either. I read somewhere that perfect is the lowest standard—because it's impossible. So aiming for perfection is like having no standard at all. Let's go into this journey knowing that we will make mistakes, but let's also go into this being kind to ourselves when they happen and make sure we learn from them. Ultimately our mistakes will make us better investors. I bet even Warren Buffett has made mistakes—and if he hadn't made any, he probably wouldn't be where he is now. The only way he wouldn't have made mistakes is if he never started investing in the first place."

She gave him a hug and a kiss on the cheek. What Maya said made complete sense, Jay thought. And looking at mistakes or setbacks as learning experiences certainly helped take away the pressure of making the right decision *all the time.* He felt relieved to embrace this mindset shift.

Still, as a high-achieving doctor, getting over his perfectionism would always be a battle for Jay, especially when it came to one of the toughest decisions to make as a new real estate investor—where to invest. If they opened the door to investing in non-local markets to diversify their portfolio, which market should they choose?

"You know, the Atlanta area is really growing," said Maya. "It actually fits all the criteria we are looking for in an investment market."

"Atlanta, huh? Well, the area is populated, so there will be plenty of options to build the right team of professionals, like property managers."

"Atlanta also has a robust and diverse economic base," Maya added. "One company moving out of the city won't totally depress it, which gives us stability and lowered risk as investors." The area was also at a relatively low risk of natural disasters. And Atlanta was fairly landlord friendly, meaning the regulations worked in property owners' favor when it came to things like evictions.

"But Atlanta also has a ton of people who have been investing there forever," Jay said. "It's a hot market with lots of competition. Maybe a little too hot."

"So what if it's a hot market?" Maya said. "That doesn't matter to me."

"Wait, what? Why's that?"

"First of all, there will always be investors out there, my love. That's not going to change. Second, people in our own course are getting deals there!" replied Maya.

"Oh that's right." Jay nodded. "That one cardiologist in Memphis just closed on a fourplex about an hour north of Atlanta and shared it with the group."

"See? Remember, there are always inefficiencies in the market. People sell individual real estate deals for lots of different reasons. Maybe it's a divorce. Maybe it's an estate sale. Maybe it's just an older owner tired of self-managing a property. Whatever the reason, there are good deals to be had out there—in any market. So, even though it's a hot market now, we can find a good deal. And when the recession comes, oh my!" laughed Maya. "We'll have our team set up and ready and just be in an amazing position to snap up deals at a discount. How does that saying go? When there's blood in the streets..."

"The time to buy is when there's blood in the streets," answered Jay. "Good points."

"And," Maya continued. "We're learning to invest in this so-called 'hot market,' so we'll have Olympic training in finding deals, which will only help us find even better deals when that recession does come. We'll probably have to *increase* our cash-on-cash return expectations when that happens. Won't that be amazing?!"

Jay clapped his hands together and gave Maya applause. "Well, dang. You are on fire! And that all makes total sense. There will be deals no matter what the market is doing. Plus, the recession will only bring more opportunities, which we'll be ready to take advantage of. So we might as well learn now, and build the team that's going to help us build a killer portfolio both now and in the future."

"Exactly."

"Alright...Atlanta it is," Jay confirmed.

"Excellent. Let's assemble our team, then."

BUILDING A TEAM

With the Atlanta area market as their target, Jay and Maya began to put together their investing team.

They had learned that building a team *before* putting in their first offer was critical. Having a team in place would help lower their risk once they had a property under contract, during the due diligence process.

Their team consisted of off-site team members and on-site team members. They were all professionals in their own right— meaning they understood their roles and were ready to offer their respective expertise when necessary. Having these team members chosen before their first offer would allow them to get the most accurate numbers and input at their first property inspection.

Off-site team members included an insurance broker, a residential lender, a commercial broker, a CPA, and an asset-protection law firm. These professionals were scattered across the country, since they didn't need to be local to Maya and Jay. Though they initially worried about not meeting with these vendors in person, Maya and Jay found that over time, their confidence grew as they built relationships with their vendors through Zoom calls and, in one case, even an in-person meeting with their commercial broker in Atlanta during a site visit.

On-site team members, who were locally based to the property, included real estate investment agents, property managers, and contractors.

Having a great property manager was a key piece of the puzzle. Once Maya and Jay found a great property manager company to handle the day-to-day responsibilities of the property, they felt much more secure in the fact that their property would be taken care of. Their property manager team was going to handle the renting of units, tenant calls and concerns, and collecting rents. They'd also take maintenance calls and handle evictions if needed. Each month they'd report the financial transactions and deposit their earnings.

With a good property manager, Jay and Maya could be as involved as they wanted to be with the running of their property. They could sit back and collect their statement, or they could actively oversee the work of the property manager. To earn enough hours to qualify for real estate professional status (REPS) and to maximize their returns, Jay planned to be actively involved in overseeing the property manager and any rehab work. To earn enough hours to qualify, Jay had also decided he would self-manage their second property independent of where it was located. Given what he had seen in the community, he knew that he had the right tools and knowledge to even self-manage properties 2,500 miles away.

Next up: investor agents. The several investor-friendly agents whom Maya and Jay interviewed in Atlanta knew the history of every neighborhood in the city—which rather impressed Maya and Jay, helping them feel even better about their decision to invest in an out-of-state area. One candidate stood out, however: Erica, a real estate investment agent who was an investor herself with several Atlanta-area properties in her own portfolio. Maya and Jay felt she was a great fit for them and decided to primarily work with her, though they didn't rule out working with other agents, especially on off-market deals that might not be available publically on the multiple listing service (MLS). Since they were actively looking for properties on the MLS themselves each day, they kept in frequent contact by emailing Erica potential deals to get her insights. Between Maya and Jay actively scouring for deals and Erica's searches and access to off-market deals/pocket listings, it was only a matter of time before they would find the right deal.

Lastly, Maya and Jay interviewed several Atlanta-area contractors. A solid contractor would help them update their units once they purchased a property. They looked for a contractor who understood rental-grade finishes and who worked primarily with rental properties. After interviewing several, Jay and Maya found a favorite with Frank, a contractor in Atlanta, from referrals through their course community. Frank had worked with several other investors in that market. Of course, during their first inspection, they'd get multiple bids from contractors, but given Frank's rave reviews, they were confident he would be a good addition to their team.

"Wow, it was a good thing we didn't get a property under contract before taking the course," Maya said, relieved. "Then we would have been scrambling trying to build a team while under contract. We would have likely made mistakes before closing without help from all these experts. That could have been a real mess. Plus, we would have been in a much weaker negotiating position during the due diligence period because we wouldn't have our experts giving us opinions about what changes to make and how much it would cost. I can't believe how blindly so many people go into this process."

"We were going into things pretty blindly, ourselves," said Jay, sheepishly. "The good news is we have a solid team in place now, though. I think we're ready to start putting in offers, eh?"

"Absolutely."

Maya and Jay both felt a sense of relief knowing that they didn't need to know all the answers, nor did they need to wear all the various hats. They had a solid team in place who could help them with that. They were ready to tackle the next step in the journey: actually buying investment properties.

LEARN MORE

While interviewing property managers is a time-consuming process, it is necessary for your success as a real estate investor. Check out our tips on how to succeed here: semiretiredmd.com/life-manager.

FINDING DEALS

Maya and Jay had built the expertise to be able to recognize and buy good deals. They could see value where others would miss it (hidden value) and had the vision of how to make that value a reality while also increasing cashflow using forced appreciation. They could run cash-on-cash calculators in their sleep. Their team was complete. They were primed and ready.

Jay and Maya had decided to target B and C properties—rather than A-class luxury buildings—because they knew the cash-on-cash return tended to be higher. These types of properties weren't newer builds with the fanciest amenities, but the type of properties that working-class people would line up to live in. They also felt secure knowing they were mitigating risk by buying these types of properties because they'd always have tenant demand, even during a recession. In fact, a downturn would likely cause rental demand to *increase* in these types of properties because as people tightened spending, they'd be more likely to choose to move into their buildings instead of high-priced type-A properties.

These properties also often contained hidden value, or opportunities to force appreciation. Maya and Jay saw opportunities for forced appreciation everywhere.

Maya and Jay could increase income to a given property by adding a storage area, renting a garage, renting parking spots, or charging pet rent. Or, they could rehab a property and rent it for a higher rate, which would both force appreciation and increase cashflow. Adding bedrooms or bathrooms to unfinished basements, for example, would also increase a property's cashflow and force appreciation.

In addition to increasing a property's income, Maya and Jay were on the lookout for ways to decrease expenses. Charging back utilities (also known as RUBS), installing low-flow showerheads and toilets to reduce water consumption, or having tenants take care of the landscaping instead of covering it could all reduce expenses and force appreciation. They also knew rehabbing decreased maintenance expenses because there would be fewer repair costs with updated units.

Maya and Jay had become experts at seeing not what a property was, but what it would become (and what it would earn and be worth to another investor) once they were done tapping all the sources of hidden value. They were excited to put their knowledge into practice with their first property.

CHECK YOUR NUMBERS

Use Semi-Retired MD's long-term rental cash-on-cash calculator to help you evaluate real estate deals.

Visit: semiretiredmd.com/life-coc

RUNNING THE NUMBERS

"Hey, check out this property that just popped up on MLS this morning," Maya said as she stirred some frothed milk into her mug, making a homemade latte. She had her laptop open on their kitchen counter and opened the listing to show Jay. It was a duplex outside of the Atlanta metro area listed for $220,000.

"I wonder if the current rents are under-market," Jay asked curiously, looking over her shoulder. "Looks like they're

$850 a unit, which seems lower than what I've seen in similar properties."

"Yeah, that seems really low," Maya said. "I've seen other two-bed/one-bath, 800-square-foot units renting for well over a thousand dollars when I've searched the rental apps—although those looked a bit nicer. And look at those last two photos. What is that?" Maya took a closer look at the property photos on the screen. "Is that a detached garage? I wonder if we could rent that separately? I just don't know for how much."

She then pulled up the satellite view. "Awesome. The garage has alleyway access, just like they taught us to look for in the course. That way a renter who doesn't live in the duplex can rent out the garage at a premium and have access through the alleyway so they don't disturb the tenants in the main building."

"Let's run the numbers on how this property is currently performing," Jay said. He got his laptop from the other room and sat down next to Maya. After finding the file on his desktop, he plugged the numbers into the long-term rental COC calculator.

Property address: Atlanta Duplex

Cash-on-Cash Return	-0.1%

Purchase Data	
Purchase Price ($)	$220,000
Down Payment (%)	25%
Closing Costs ($)	$2,500
Repairs/Renovation ($)	$0
Loan Data	
Amount Financed ($)	$165,000
Interest Rate (%)	5.25%
Years	30
Payments per Year	12
Property Data	
Number of Units	2
Property Taxes/Year ($)	$1,400
Insurance/Year ($)	$1,200
Monthly Gross Rental Income ($)	$1,700
Vacancy Rate (%)	5%
Property Management Data	
Property Management Fee (%)	8%
Leasing Cost per Unit ($)	$500
Average Occupancy (years)	1
Maintenance Costs (%)	5%
Monthly Utilities/Other	$200

Monthly Net Operating Income	
Gross Rental Income	$1,700
Average Vacancy	$85
Net Rental Income	$1,615
Property Management	$129
Leasing	$83
Maintenance	$85
Utilities	$200
Property Taxes	$117
Insurance	$100
Expenses	$714
Net Operating Income	$901

Monthly/Annual Cashflow	Monthly	Annual
Net Operating Income	$901	
Principal and Interest	$907	
Cashflow	($6)	($76)

Total Investment	
Down Payment	$55,000
Closing Costs	$2,500
Repairs/Renovation	$0
	$57,500

Property of Semi-Retired MD

"Ouch," Jay said once he finished. "It's getting a *negative* 0.1 percent return. If we bought it at this price, we'd lose around $76 a year, assuming a modest vacancy rate, a 5 percent maintenance cost per year, and our other fixed costs."

"Yikes," said Maya. "That's bad. But, remember, it's not what it's doing right now, but what it'll do once we own it. Let's ask Abby what she thinks about the rent. Maybe she'll tell us they're undermarket, just like we suspect."

Jay texted the listing over to their property manager in Atlanta to get her opinion. Abby confirmed the rent was way under market value, and though she wasn't exactly sure about the garage rental since her team had never rented one, she had heard of other property managers renting double garages for $150–$200 a month. She also mentioned the rents could probably increase $150–$200 more per month per unit with a few small upgrades like new flooring, paint, and some kitchen improvements.

"Talk about hidden value," Jay said excitedly. "We could also bill back utilities. I know we can do that in the Atlanta area because I've seen other members in the membership community doing it. All in all, that should increase the property's income by at least $600 a month over what it's producing now."

Maya and Jay contacted the rest of their team members to help confirm the variables in their cash-on-cash calculator. Their lender let them know what the current interest rate would be on the loan, and their insurance broker gave them some rough estimates on insurance costs in their market based on the square footage of the property. They also called the city to confirm what the new property taxes would be after they purchased the property if they bought it at the listing price. The city reported that property taxes would increase by about $150 a year.

Based on this information, and the increased rent potential, the potential garage rental, and the utility bill backs (RUBS), Jay and Maya did what the course taught them to do next—to go back to their cash-on-cash calculator for a second time to see how the property would perform after they were done improving it. They started plugging in some prospective numbers.

"How much should we put in for repairs and renovation?" Jay asked.

"I don't know. I'll ask the community, though. Maybe they can give us a ballpark amount based on their prior experience."

"Good idea. I'll shoot a text to our agent, too. Since she owns properties herself, she might have a sense of what rehabbing two-bed/one-bath units costs."

"And while you're at it, why not ask Abby, too?" Maya suggested. "That way, we can triangulate the data. Whatever the number ends up being, I think we should stay more on the conservative side." As Jay texted their team members, Maya's question was already getting responses from their online community.

"It looks like rehab costs range between $10,000 to $15,000 per unit from our fellow doctors," Maya said.

Jay's phone buzzed. "Our agent said something similar. She estimated between $12,000 to $15,000." His phone buzzed again. "That must be Abby...Yep. She said between $7,000 and $10,000."

"Let's use the higher end of the spectrum for now," Maya suggested. "Let's put $15,000 for each unit, plus the garage will likely need some updating, too. Let's add $5,000 for that space. So that's an estimated $35,000 in repairs/renovations. We will get the real numbers later, after the inspection, but I'd rather put a higher number in now and be pleasantly surprised later when it's lower!"

"Good call," Jay said as he finished entering the numbers. "We can get a 8.8 percent return after increasing rents, renting the garage, billing back utilities, and updating the interior."

"Hey! That's a huge improvement! But that's still not 10 percent, like we initially talked about as our goal."

"Since it isn't quite there, do you think we shouldn't make an offer?" asked Jay.

"Well..." Maya trailed off as she thought about it. After a minute, she looked at Jay. "I think we should still put in an offer. This is why: First, it's really close to our target of 10 percent at 8.8 percent cash-on-cash return. What if we find out that rents can go up an extra fifty dollars a month per unit after the inspection? That would get us closer to 10 percent. And even if that doesn't happen, my bet is, in a year or two, we can raise rents to get us to 10 percent—or even higher.

"That's true," Jay said.

She continued. "Second, we could be off on our rehab numbers. What if it only costs $7,000 to rehab each unit? Then our cash-on-cash return will definitely bump up. Third, it's great practice for us to start putting in offers. We might not get it, and that's fine, but we'll at least learn from the experience. Plus, if our offer is accepted, then this is going to be an amazing opportunity for us to look for ways to make the COC return even higher than we think is possible right now. I think it will challenge us to come up with other creative ways to boost the cash-on-cash. Worst case, we find out the deal doesn't work for us, we'll lose some money through the inspection, but we would have learned a lot, and this will be part of the cost of our education."

"Solid points, love—and I'm with you. Plus, if we put in an offer with our agent, she'll see we're serious. We'll get to go through the process and learn about how it is working, together."

"Exactly. How many times have we seen examples of people putting in offers that didn't work out only for them to stumble upon another deal a week or two later? You never know what's around the corner."

"Absolutely," Jay said. "Let's do it. Let's see what Erica thinks about the neighborhood, too." He sent the listing via text. "If she's on board, let's move forward fast to get it under contract."

Their agent confirmed the property looked like a great deal in an up-and-coming area. She expected that there would be other offers given the sales price. Maya and Jay couldn't wait. It was time to act. This was the moment they had been working for.

"Are you ready to do this?" Jay asked.

"Yes! Let's put in our offer before anyone else jumps on this opportunity."

Maya and Jay immediately put in their offer at full price in an effort to get the property locked up, under contract, and off the market before any other investor had a chance.

CHAPTER 8

THE FIRST PURCHASE

"Rich people acquire assets. The poor and middle class acquire liabilities that they think are assets."

—ROBERT KIYOSAKI

"Hey, Maya!"

"Yes, love?"

"Guess what? They accepted our offer!"

"Wow, that was quick!" Maya did a gleeful silly dance. "It's finally happening!"

Within three hours of putting in their offer on the duplex outside of Atlanta, Jay and Maya had locked it up, meaning they got the property under contract. They got it because they had moved faster than any other investor, and the seller had agreed to their offer before other, higher offers had rolled in the following day.

"I have to admit, as exciting as this is, I'm also feeling a bit nervous about it, Maya," Jay admitted as he paced around the kitchen. "We're doing this from so far away...how can we really trust this is a good deal? What if it ends up being a money pit?"

"Jay, remember that our team down there knows what they're doing a lot more than we do," Maya said. "I mean, our agent has been working in that community forever. She knows every block, she's seen the market go up and down, she knows which neighborhoods are progressing. She assured us this looks like a good deal to her. We've checked the numbers ourselves. Our team members will let us know during the inspection if they see something concerning. We have multiple experts giving us their opinions, we'll do our own assessment, and we have the community who can weigh in, too. We can always negotiate a price reduction if anything is found during inspection—or even walk away if the deal doesn't work. All we've done by locking it up is secure the opportunity to buy the property if everything checks out. We don't actually own it yet!"

"But shouldn't we go down there to watch the inspection?" Jay asked anxiously. "It just feels so weird to make a decision about a property costing hundreds of thousands of dollars without even setting foot in it."

"We already discussed this," replied Maya confidently. "Even if you could get the days off from clinic on such short notice, what are we going to do by being there? Walk around and nod as people tell us what they're seeing? What would change if we are there in person rather than on a video call? Nothing that I can see. Ultimately it comes down to our agent, property manager, inspector, and contractor giving us their advice as experts. And plugging in the numbers. We've vetted all of them through the community. I feel secure in how they've shown up so far."

Jay nodded. He placed his hands on his head and took a deep breath. "And the community has our backs. If we run across anything we're unsure of, we can ask in there and get their perspective."

"In the end, though, this is all about the numbers" reminded Maya. "We are investors; we buy only when the numbers make sense. Listen, if this deal works out, let's make the time to go down to Atlanta next month to check out the property and meet our team. In the meantime, if we ever feel uncomfortable with what's going on, we'll make sure to get other opinions—from other property managers or contractors and the community—to make sure we cover all our bases and reduce our risk as much as possible using data triangulation. Everything will be fine!"

Jay closed his eyes, took a deep breath, and exhaled audibly through his mouth. Maya was right. He decided that rather than anxiety, an emotion that would serve him better was excitement. He therefore focused on how much he would learn through this process and how much better investors they'd be after, whether they ended up buying the deal or not.

THE INSPECTION

Five days after their offer was accepted, inspection day arrived. The night before, Maya and Jay reviewed the numbers again.

"This property is currently getting a negative 0.1 percent cash-on-cash return if we buy it at the offer price," Jay said.

"But it's owned by mom-and-pop landlords who haven't made upgrades in years, at least from the looks of the photos," Maya said. "Let's ask Abby and the contractors tomorrow what select upgrades we should make to further increase rents. Let's also make sure the contractors give us a worst case scenario bid for any repairs that need to be made so we can use it during negotiations. This will also help us build the most conservative COC return calculations."

"Let's also make sure we understand what we need to do to make the garage rentable and how much that will cost," Jay said. You're going to have to take the lead since I will be at clinic tomorrow. But I can join you on FaceTime and try to listen in between patients. The way we've calculated our cash-on-cash calculator to get the 8.8 percent cash-on-cash right now assumes that we can increase rents by $600 and completely bill back utilities."

"I can't believe we might own this property in less than a month!" Maya squealed.

"It's been a long time coming," Jay said. "But remember, we're investors. We make decisions based on the numbers, not emotions."

"You sound just like someone I know," laughed Maya. "Good thing the numbers are looking good, though!"

"They are...for now. Let's get some rest. Tomorrow is a big day for us."

The next day, Erica, their real estate investor agent, got Maya and Jay on separate video call lines as the rest of their team assembled outside the property, including their contractor, property manager, and inspector.

"Hi everyone!" Erica said. "Thanks for being there to walk the property today." She introduced the team members to each other and then focused on Maya and Jay. Maya sat at their kitchen table with her iPad on the counter and her laptop nearby with access to their online doctor community for support, if she needed it. Jay was on his phone at work, but planned to be intermittently checking in between seeing patients.

While their team members dispersed to start their work, Erica turned to talk directly to Maya and Jay on her screen.

"So what's going to happen today, Maya and Jay, is we are going to walk the property together on the phone. Then, once the inspector has gone through the property, he'll call you later to cover any major issues that need to be fixed. For example, maybe the water heater is near the end of its life, or there's siding that needs to be replaced. You'll also get a full written report from the inspector by email in the next couple of days, which we can review together for any potential red flags to use during negotiations with the sellers."

"Alright, sounds good," Maya said.

"It's great you have multiple contractors here today to provide insight into how much any repairs may cost. I also think it's smart that you've arranged for your property manager to stop by to weigh in on how any rehab or improvements might affect rent. Once we have a full picture from the inspector, your property manager, and multiple contractor bids, we'll have a much better idea of what needs to be repaired and upgraded. We will also be in a better position to negotiate with the sellers and ultimately determine if you want to move forward and buy this property."

Erica then started touring them around the outside of the building on her phone. Immediately, concerning sights appeared on Jay and Maya's screens.

"That roof looks like it's in pretty rough shape," said Jay. "I wonder if it's going to need to be replaced?"

"I think so," Erica confirmed. "Let's see what the inspector and contractor think, though. If it does, we can ask for that to be done when we go back with our inspection response."

The team opened the door and went inside. Jay and Maya were mortified at the condition of the units.

"Ooh, my," Maya said under her breath, suddenly feeling nervous. "Look at those carpets. They are so stained. Some of those cabinet doors are falling off—wait. Are those burn spots on the counter?"

She looked at Jay with wide eyes. "I can't believe someone is living there."

As they continued on their video tour with their agent, Maya took to her laptop and typed a message to the course's online community: "We're in the middle of our inspection and this was *not* what we were expecting. The kitchen in this place looks awful—the cabinets are falling apart, the carpet is disgusting! There's even mold in the bathroom. We're feeling pretty nervous and having second thoughts."

Immediately, responses to her post started coming in.

"Same thing happened to me," wrote one student. "I was shocked at the state of my first property. But cleaning the place up and painting can make a big difference!"

"You'd be surprised what new floors and counters, and some fresh paint on the cabinets can do," read another. "I know it looks scary when you're new, but it's usually just cosmetic work."

Their team at the property had a similar response.

"This is actually in pretty decent shape," said Frank, their contractor. "I think the cabinets can stay, some paint and new hardware will make a big difference. The appliances are working, so those can stay. The bathroom is in decent condition. You'll need a venting fan to prevent mold. Removing the mold is minor—probably less than $500. Painting the bathroom vanity and refinishing the tub will make a big impact, too. So you'd be looking at replacing the floors throughout, new kitchen countertops, new lighting fixtures, and just repainting everything."

"Luxury vinyl plank [LVP] is the standard flooring in rental units around here," Abby chimed in. "I agree, some paint on the cabinets and those upgrades, and this place will rent well. I think we could get $200 more per unit per month—so probably around $1,050 per unit.

She addressed the garage next: "Although we've never rented garages ourselves before," Abby admitted, "I've looked around and seen a lot of similar garages to what you have here renting for $200 a month to people who want to use it as storage for cars or wood shops and things like that. I feel pretty confident that if we run electricity to the garage, we could get a solid $200 a month. Plus, the garage renter should cover the electricity costs each month."

Jay and Maya felt better after everyone's responses. They felt relieved to hear they weren't the only ones who were a bit shocked at the state of their first property, felt reassured by everyone's opinions that everything was a fairly easy fix, and felt confident in their team members' expertise.

But the inspection wasn't over yet. Their team headed downstairs to the unfinished basement of the first unit. Erica followed them with Maya and Jay tagging along on video.

"Wow," the contractor said. "These ceilings are really high for a basement. It's rare to find seven-foot ceilings in these spaces. You could put a couple bedrooms and a bathroom down here."

"That'd double the size of these units, taking you from a two-bed/one-bath to a four-bed/two-bath," said Abby. "So you can expect rent to go up significantly. Tenants are currently paying $850/month, and while I mentioned $1,050 a month with the upstairs fixed up, if you built out this basement by adding two bedrooms and a bathroom, you may be able to increase rent to between $1,300 to $1,400 a month."

"Talk about hidden value," Jay said, raising his eyebrows as he looked at Maya on his screen.

"Well that's good news," said Maya. "But how much is this all going to cost?"

"I'll draw you up a bid and get it to you in a day or two," Frank said. "That'll tell you what kind of rehab costs you're looking at for each of the options."

"And I'll use my rent comparison software to confirm the final estimates on the rent increase based on each scenario we discussed," added Abby.

"Okay, thank you all so much," said Maya. "We'll chat soon." Erica hung up but Maya and Jay stayed on the video call to talk. "What do you think, Jay?"

"Definitely not what I was expecting, but there's a bit of good news with the basement, no?"

"Yeah, I am a little shocked at the condition of that property, to be honest. I'm going to post some pictures to our group," Maya said.

"Good idea. While you do that, I have a patient to see. I'll be right back," Jay said. He left his phone at his station while he attended to his patient.

"Just finished the inspection," Maya wrote to their doctor community. "Jay and I are still a little dismayed at what we saw. The place needs a lot of work!" She attached some pictures.

As she waited, Jay finished with his patient and joined her back on the call. "Hi. I'm back. Any responses yet?"

"Actually, yes," Maya said. She read them out loud to Jay.

"Let the numbers, not your fears, guide your decision," wrote one fellow student. "Just get your bid from your contractor, then go back to your cash-on-cash calculator and make sure the numbers still work. If they don't work, renegotiate. If the seller won't agree to what you need, you don't have to move forward with the deal."

"I walked away from my first deal because my numbers *didn't* work," wrote another student. "Trust your numbers and don't make emotional decisions. It's an investment, not a home purchase!"

"I have to keep reminding myself that we can always walk away from the deal. I find great comfort in that," said Jay. "So, Maya, what do you think about tackling such a big rehab project out of the gate? I can see that the forced appreciation would be huge if we added those extra bedrooms and bathrooms downstairs if the rents really increase as much as the property manager is thinking. I mean, this property could easily be worth maybe even a couple hundred thousand dollars more after just a few months of rehab. But it'd be a pretty big project to take on, wouldn't it? Do we think we could manage a huge project like this from afar?"

"Well," said Maya, rubbing her head, "I've seen other people in the community successfully do it. There's also additional training on doing rehabs that I haven't watched on the membership site, so I'm sure we could learn more there. We have a stellar team. Frank has also worked with several others in the community on fairly large projects, and comes highly recommended, so even though it's our first purchase, I think I'd probably be up for it. If we could increase the value of the property by even $100,000, it means we could maybe do what all those other students are doing with pulling the equity out and reusing it to buy another property. What's that called again?"

"Oh, you mean a cash-out refinance? It *would* be nice to increase the property's value and then pull that equity out to reuse on our next purchase. If we do that, we won't run through our savings so quickly. And imagine what buying another extra property this year would mean to our growth! For now, though, we just need to be patient and wait to get the contractor bids and final property manager numbers. Then we can plug in all the scenarios into our cash-on-cash calculator and see what works."

"That's true," Maya said. "Let's wait to get all the final numbers."

"Ok, love, I gotta run. I have another patient," Jay said. "I'll see you tonight."

While they waited for the contractor's bid to come in, Maya started performing other due diligence tasks for the property. This included reviewing all of the leases for the current tenants to confirm they were paying what the seller said they were paying for rent—and on time. For this property, all of the listing information was accurate and none of the tenants were behind in rent, much to Maya's relief.

THE NUMBERS COME IN

Within two days of the inspection, Jay and Maya received multiple contractor bids for the rehab of their property.

"It's going to be about $15,000 to replace the roof," read Jay.

"And what about the rehab?"

"Adding the bedrooms and bathroom downstairs, and doing the kitchen upgrades and paint upstairs—so everything—is coming in at $60,000 with Frank."

"Oh, wow," Maya gasped. "That's way more than what we anticipated. We went from an estimated $35,000 in renovation to $75,000? That's a massive increase!"

"Yes, but that was before the inspection. And hold on, let me finish the rest of the report. Rent could go from $850 per month to $1,400 per month reliably—if we added those two bedrooms and a bathroom to the downstairs basement. If we don't do the basement rehab, then the estimate is $1,050 a month for rent."

"Ok, so we could get $2,800 in rental income if we finished the basement, plus the $200 a month for the garage. That's $3,000 a month total."

"Correct. And remember, we could also renegotiate to get the roof covered by the seller, based on its condition."

"That's true," Maya said. "We could also decide not to do the downstairs upgrade, which would save us $30,000. Let's plug the numbers into the COC calculator for both scenarios. First, can you plug in the numbers if we decided *not* to do the downstairs rehab?"

"Sure. So, if we didn't tackle the basement, our rehab costs would be $45,000—$30,000 for the upstairs update and then $15,000 for the roof. That would mean we could charge $1,050 in rent...plus $200 a month in garage rent..." Jay finished plugging in the numbers. "That would give us a 7.9 percent cash-on-cash return."

"Well, that's not what we want," Maya said, scrunching up her face. "Okay, now plug in the numbers if we did the downstairs rehab, thereby increasing rents."

Jay spoke the numbers out loud as he plugged them in. "$75,000 for rehab...then $3,000 for rent...oh wow! Our cash-on-cash return would increase to 11.3 percent!"

"Hey! That's incredible...but that's still spending $75,000 in rehab costs. What would it look like if we had the seller replace the roof?"

Jay took out the $15,000 for the roof, and plugged in $60,000 for the estimated rehab of both the downstairs, upstairs, and garage.

"Wowza," Jay remarked. "If we could get the seller to cover the roof, we'd get a 12.8 percent return!"

"That type of cash-on-cash return would be killer—especially for our first property!" She gave Jay a high-five. "Let's definitely see if we can go back to the seller and put the roof on him. If this deal falls through, he'll have to disclose the roof needs to be replaced to the next seller anyway. He knows that. So hopefully he'll be motivated to negotiate."

"We can also ask for a reduction in the overall price. The place needed a lot more TLC coming out of the inspection than what the listing indicated."

They called Erica to discuss. With her help, Maya and Jay not only asked the seller to replace the roof before closing, but they also asked the seller to reduce the price by $10,000 to cover some of the issues uncovered during the inspection.

After a bit of back and forth, the seller agreed to replacing the roof and to lowering the sales price by $5,000, which slightly decreased the property taxes and insurance amounts. Jay and Maya took their updated numbers back to their cash-on-cash calculator to make the final decision on whether they would move forward with purchasing this property.

Property address: Atlanta Duplex

Cash-on-Cash Return	13.2%

Purchase Data	
Purchase Price ($)	$215,000
Down Payment (%)	25%
Closing Costs ($)	$2,500
Repairs/Renovation ($)	$60,000
Loan Data	
Amount Financed ($)	$161,250
Interest Rate (%)	5.25%
Years	30
Payments per Year	12
Property Data	
Number of Units	2
Property Taxes/Year ($)	$1,525
Insurance/Year ($)	$1,195
Monthly Gross Rental Income ($)	$3,000
Vacancy Rate (%)	5%
Property Management Data	
Property Management Fee (%)	8%
Leasing Cost per Unit ($)	$500
Average Occupancy (years)	1
Maintenance Costs (%)	5%
Monthly Utilities/Other	$0

Monthly Net Operating Income	
Gross Rental Income	$3,000
Average Vacancy	$150
Net Rental Income	$2,850
Property Management	$228
Leasing	$83
Maintenance	$150
Utilities	$0
Property Taxes	$127
Insurance	$100
Expenses	$688
Net Operating Income	$2,162

Monthly/Annual Cashflow		
	Monthly	Annual
Net Operating Income	$2,162	
Principal and Interest	$887	
Cashflow	$1,275	$15,305

Total Investment	
Down Payment	$53,750
Closing Costs	$2,500
Repairs/Renovation	$60,000
	$116,250

"After our negotiation, we're looking at a 13.2 percent cash-on-cash return!" Jay confirmed.

"And we'll get more than $15,000 in cashflow annually! This is phenomenal!"

In addition, after rehabbing and making the duplex a four-bed/two-bath, Erica felt it was likely the property would appraise close to $400,000. At that point, Maya and Jay could do a cash-out refi after and reuse the funds again to buy another property.

"Talk about a good deal!" Jay exclaimed. "Even if our rehab runs over by 10 percent or even 20 percent, we'll be fine."

"I'll say!" Maya squealed. "And it started out at only 8.8 percent cash-on-cash return. Look at us using the options we had at hand to increase the cash-on-cash return even beyond our initial goal! Go us!"

"So we're buying it, right?" asked Jay.

"Ahhh, YES!" shouted Maya. They let the inspection contingency on their contract expire. They were one step closer to owning their first investment property!

THE APPRAISAL

After the inspection contingency expired, Maya and Jay had to wait an additional two weeks for the appraisal. The appraisal was ordered by the bank to find out how much the property was valued at the time of purchase. This step was required before the bank funded Jay and Maya's loan.

"What if the appraisal comes back lower than the sale price?" Maya asked. "Then we can't get our loan and the whole deal could fall through. I don't like waiting! It feels like forever."

"I know, I feel that way, too," said Jay. They once again turned to their peers in the community to give them some perspective.

"We're anxiously waiting on the appraisal for our first property—emphasis on the anxious part," Maya wrote on the community page. "Can anyone share their experiences with the appraisal contingency?"

"I was scared that my first property wouldn't appraise," wrote one fellow doctor. "But then I was reminded that if the appraisal comes back low, it's just another opportunity to negotiate. You can ask for a price reduction from the seller."

"We've negotiated a lower sale price because of a low appraisal," wrote another. "The seller was already three weeks into the process, they just wanted the sale done, so they gave us what we asked for."

"Yes, remember, it all comes down to the numbers," wrote a third. "Whatever comes your way, you can handle it. And if it doesn't work out, you can always walk away from the deal."

The support made Jay and Maya feel better while they waited for the appraisal value.

Jay's phone let out its notification chime for a new email. "The appraisal came back at $245,000!" he exclaimed as he read the email from their agent. "Look, we already made $30,000 at the time of purchase. Now *that's* a good deal—getting immediate appreciation on day one!"

They both laughed and breathed a huge sigh of relief as their appraisal contingency expired.

LEARN MORE

Contingencies are an important part of the buying process for rental properties. To learn more, visit semiretiredmd.com/life-contingencies.

ANOTHER OPPORTUNITY POPS UP

Maya and Jay had used $53,750 of their $150,000 savings for the down payment on the Atlanta duplex, but after including closing costs, it was closer to $56,000. They technically had enough saved to pay for the $60,000 rehab, but that plan changed about a week before close, when Maya saw a new opportunity pop up on Redfin. It was a duplex for sale in their home state of Washington.

"What if, instead of doing the rehab with the money we already have, we just go buy another property?" Maya suggested playfully one Saturday morning. "To make up the difference, we can borrow from our 401(k) to do the rehab. I think we can borrow $50,000. That way, our money goes further."

Jay stared blankly at Maya. "Don't you think it's a little crazy to jump into a second property so soon?"

"I don't think so. After everything we've learned and all the knowledge we've gained about real estate investing, I feel pretty confident in what we've done so far. Remember, we are way ahead of most real estate investors by taking a course. Look how much we've learned. Plus we have a community who help us see situations from multiple perspectives and keep us from making a lot of mistakes. I feel pretty good about diving in again, even though it does seem sort of fast."

"It does look like a good deal," Jay said, reviewing the Redfin listing. "And I want to self-manage our second property. Having one so close would help me get the hours I need for real estate professional status this year. Maybe I'll even do some of the rehab?"

"If you want to," Maya said. "I can definitely see how that would help rack up hours and reduce some costs."

They both paused for a moment, thinking about all they had learned.

"We have the skill set now to just keep building our portfolio one property at a time," Maya finally said, breaking the silence. "We can do this to make money for the rest of our lives. It's pretty amazing when you think about it. We have financial skills now—we know how to make money. These are skills we can even pass down to our kids when we have them!"

"It *is* pretty amazing. Nothing can hold us back now," laughed Jay.

With that confidence, Maya and Jay decided to put in an offer for the second property. With the help of their investor-friendly lender, who assured them they could secure two residential loans at once, they locked up their second property while still in the process of closing on their first. And just like that, they'd entered two markets in a matter of weeks.

HOUSE HACKING

As they were in the process of doing their due diligence on the Washington property, Jay and Maya also started to explore house hacking.

"Some real estate investors buy multifamily properties with low money down—for example, they use a doctor loan to buy a small multifamily property, like a fourplex—and then they live in one unit of the property and rent out the others," Jay explained. "So they live rent free. Living for free in a property that you're renting is called house hacking."

"For what we are paying in rent right now," Maya chimed in, "that would save us enough to make another down payment on a property this year. Plus, I really like the idea that we could put less money down since it'd be our primary residence. That would help our money go further with down payments on other properties. How much do you think we'd have to put down, Jay?"

"I'm not sure," he admitted. "I've heard of some people putting down just 3.5 percent using FHA loans, but I don't think we'd be able to get one of those. But even if we could put 10 percent down, it'd make a big difference, because we'd have more cash left over to fix the place up. Ideally we house hack a property we can rehab, too. The upgrades we'd make would add a lot more value to the property."

"Oh smart! We could force a lot of appreciation."

"Exactly. After rehabbing the property and forcing appreciation, we could also do a cash-out refinance. That's when we replace our current loan with a new one based on the property's new value, and get the difference back in cash for our next purchase."

Maya laughed. "I think you're a little addicted to buying cash-flowing rental properties!"

A beaming smile spread across Jay's face. "I am! I'm constantly surfing Redfin looking for our next deal. I love the idea of doing a house hack to make our money go further, and then doing a cash-out refi to buy our next property. But we don't even have to house hack. We can do a cash-out refi on our current properties if we want to, once they're rehabbed."

"Oh really?"

"Yep, like I mentioned a couple days ago, we could do a cash-out refi with the property we're buying right now. Once we rehab it and increase rents, it's going to be worth a lot more. That's that forced appreciation for you. Then we can get another appraisal, and get a new loan, and then use the same money to buy our next property. We could do this over and over again. That way, we would essentially be reusing the same money to buy property after property. I've seen lots of people do this in the community. Like they say, every real estate investor runs out of money eventually. But that's when cash-out refis and other advanced financing strategies come into play."

"That's actually pretty brilliant. That would allow us to grow our portfolio without starting with *that* much money."

"That's right. Plus, when we get our tax refund check next year thanks to me having real estate professional status, we could add that to the mix, and afford bigger properties and take on bigger rehab projects."

They decided the Washington property that Jay had been eyeing wasn't the right one for them to house hack, but it was definitely something they'd consider doing if the right property showed up down the road.

"Let's keep our eyes open for house hacking opportunities," said Maya.

LEARN MORE

Want to learn more about house hacking? Check out our own hacking experience by visiting semiretiredmd.com/life-househacking.

THE CLOSING

Finally, after about thirty days of having the property under contract and working through the various contingencies, the day had come for Jay and Maya to close on the Atlanta duplex. A mobile notary came to their house, and they signed the paperwork in their kitchen.

After they signed their names and took signing pics to post in their online community, they looked at each other, triumphantly.

"We're officially real estate investors!" Maya cheered.

"This calls for wine," said Jay, searching the cabinet for a bottle. He poured them each a glass.

"I can't believe how far we've come," Maya remarked. "We officially own a rental property—in Atlanta of all places! And we're about to own another one right here in Washington." She smiled. All the worry about that first deal was worth it. They had learned a tremendous amount and had gained a lot of confidence in their knowledge as real estate investors.

"And we're just getting started," said Jay, holding up his glass.

"Exactly." Maya clinked her glass with his. "We are *just* getting started."

CHAPTER 9

YOU WIN SOME, YOU *LEARN* SOME

"You should never view your challenges as a disadvantage. Instead, it's important for you to understand that your experience facing and overcoming adversity is actually one of your biggest advantages."

—MICHELLE OBAMA

Three months after tenants moved into the Atlanta complex, the property manager called Jay.

"Hey, Abby, how's it going?"

"Hey, Jay. Ugh. I have some bad news."

"Uh, oh. What happened?"

"Well, I stopped by to replace one of the outdoor lights that burnt out earlier this week, and I was met with some more wannabe art on the side of the building."

"Graffiti? Again? I thought we just cleaned some up?

"We did, but apparently that was not appreciated. I'll send you photos. The good news is that it looks smaller than before, so the cleanup shouldn't cost any more than we spent last time."

Jay dropped his head back to look up at the ceiling and sighed deeply. "Well, thanks for the call. Yes, please get it cleaned up. Hopefully this doesn't happen again." He hung up the phone.

"We got more graffiti?" Maya asked.

"Yep, sounds like it."

Someone first vandalized the side of their building only weeks after the rehab was finished. When Abby called to tell them about it, Jay and Maya had frustratingly given the okay to spend $250 to remove it.

"I can't believe someone would do that—twice, no less!" Jay said. "I feel almost violated, especially after all the money and effort we put in to improve that building. It's such a cleaner, safer place to live. Our tenants love it. I mean, who does something like this?"

"You can't let it get to you, love."

"I know, I know," Jay said, even though he was still upset about it. "It's just...annoying. Like come on! We shouldn't have to deal with things like this."

"Oh trust me, I don't want to have to deal with it either," Maya said. "But I try to look at it through a more positive lens. Things like that are going to happen. If we ask: 'How is this life happening for us?' then maybe the answer is this is training us to be persistent and stay focused on the big things, not worry about these little things, you know? It's only $250."

"Well, I don't want any training on being persistent!" grumbled Jay. "But yeah, you're right. I mean, when I remind myself that we're building a multimillion-dollar real estate portfolio here, something tiny like graffiti isn't going to matter in five years. Future Jay is not concerned with this, so present Jay should not be either," he said with a slight laugh.

"When you start talking about yourself in the third person, I get a little worried," teased Maya. "But in this case, future Jay is right: let's focus our energy on things that serve us and keep building. This is just a tiny tiny speed bump along the way."

REHAB REVIEW

With the Atlanta property, Maya and Jay had embarked on their first rehab of an investment property. They'd added two bedrooms and a bathroom to the downstairs of both units. Remarkably, the entire thing had gone smoother than expected, especially considering they had so much initial fear doing everything from afar.

They were grateful for the team they'd built in that market before even putting in their offer. They had hired seasoned experts who called Jay and Maya and kept them updated on every detail of the project, while being careful not to overwhelm them. They provided practical solutions based on years of experience for Maya and Jay to approve. A permitting issue, for example, required that they open walls in two different areas—twice! But with each call, their team had suggestions about how to best solve the problem and stepped in to get the work done.

As the rehab came to a close, the property manager started screening tenants—and boy, was there demand. Lots of families inquired about the property, which made Maya and Jay realize what else this venture was providing: an actual nice place to live for others.

"Is it just me, or do you have the fuzzies?" Maya asked Jay after a video meeting with Abby.

"The fuzzies? What do you mean?"

"You know...the warm and fuzzies. We own a place people *want* to live in. Did you see how many applicants we got? It's unreal, but also heartwarming. I feel pretty proud that we aren't slumlords, but property investors who care about providing a safe, clean, updated place for our tenants to live in."

"Oh yes—those fuzzies! I definitely didn't expect to feel this good about this part of the process."

Meanwhile, Jay had been self-managing the couple's local property in Washington so he could meet the criteria to obtain real estate professional status. The closing had gone smoothly and rehabbing was nearing its close. While they had felt in the loop every step of the way with the Atlanta rehab, they had learned even more witnessing the week-to-week rehab progress with their self-managed Washington duplex firsthand.

Despite racking up hours at their two properties, Jay still needed more to qualify for real estate professional status that year, which meant they needed to buy another property so he could put in some serious hours before the tax year ended.

"Hey Maya, check out this fourplex on Lincoln Street," said Jay one morning while drinking his coffee and reviewing listings for their potential third property. "It's not too far from our duplex. It looks too good to pass up."

"Ooof. Look at those photos! That place definitely needs a face-lift, but that just means there's a lot of opportunity to force some appreciation, right?!" she said looking over his shoulder at his computer screen. "It's just...well...where are we going to get the funds for the down payment?"

"Well, I think it's time to do a cash-out refi," suggested Jay. "Since the Atlanta duplex rehab is done, I think we've forced enough appreciation to pull money out of it to use to purchase this new one."

"Oooo, yes. The value on that property has to be close to $350,000 now, and we only purchased it for $215,000. By replacing the current loan with a new one, we should be able to get enough cash out for a down payment on the next property."

"Let's do it," Jay said. "I'll call our lender to get the loan terms. I know the interest rate has bumped up since we bought it, but I think the numbers will still work well. We'll be adding another property to our portfolio in no time."

CASH-OUT REFI PAYS OFF

A few weeks later, Maya phoned Jay as she headed out of the hospital after a weeklong shift.

"Hey, love," she said. "We are scheduled Thursday morning for the mobile notary to come over so we can close on the refi. I want to go over the numbers once more to make sure we're all set:

- "Our rehab on the Atlanta duplex forced enough appreciation that the property is now appraising at $375,000—more than we initially thought!
- "We'll do a cash-out refi on the new valuation and get a new loan at 70 percent of that, so we'll get $262,500 out of the property.
- "We'll pay off the old loan, which is now $156,250 since we paid off some of the principal this last year.
- "That'll leave us with roughly $100,000 to use for the Lincoln Street property.

"Does that make sense? Did I miss anything?" Maya asked. She'd reached her car and was now reviewing the numbers on the piece of paper propped up on her steering wheel.

"Makes sense to me," said Jay. "I want that fourplex on Lincoln Street. It's a great deal. This will also mean over another $10,000 in cashflow per year, not to mention the tax savings, forced appreciation, renters paying down the mortgage..." His voice trailed off.

Once Maya and Jay purchased the property, they would have eight doors, securing Jay plenty of hours of work to comfortably claim real estate professional status for the year.

"Once we get the Lincoln Street fourplex up and running, we will have achieved all of our real estate goals for the year! How awesome is that?"

"It's amazing," laughed Maya. "We really made our plan a reality this year!"

THE FOUR-LETTER WORD: DEBT

"Are you worried about being over leveraged?" Jay asked Maya one evening over dinner a couple days away from closing on their third property. "So many of our colleagues are trying to get out of debt. They are paying off their student loans as fast as they can. Some are even trying to pay off their loans on their primary residences. Yet, here we are actively adding debt to purchase multiple properties this year. Does that stress you out?"

They'd discussed it before, but as doctors with thousands of dollars in outstanding student loans, debt was always on their minds.

"Yes and no," answered Maya. "Logically, I know we are using debt to build wealth. Plus, we have the cushion of cashflow, our renters are paying down our mortgages, we have tax savings, we are adding value to the property by forcing appreciation, and we have the possibility of market appreciation. All these things are going to increase our net worth quickly, precisely because we are using leverage and willing to incur debt right now.

"And when you're aiming to build wealth quickly, debt is usually necessary, despite being taught our whole lives that debt is bad," she continued. "I don't consider what we're doing as collecting bad debt—it's not like we are buying a Lamborghini or some other liability. What we have is good debt—debt used to buy assets. I know that the wealthy use debt to grow their net worth, too, so we are in good company."

"But doesn't the idea of having hundreds of thousands of additional debt by the end of this year freak you out?" Jay pushed. "Every time I think about it, I feel my blood pressure rise." He looked a little ill.

"I mean, yes," admitted Maya. "But then I remind myself that the alternatives are not okay, either. I won't sit here and continue to just rely on our jobs as our only source of income. That's risky, too. And I'm not willing to spend the rest of my life working so hard in medicine, never seeing you or having time with our future children. I'm not willing to live my life that way."

"Neither am I," said Jay. "And I don't want to wait to save up for years to pay for each property with cash, either. Our growth would be so much slower. I wouldn't get real estate professional status this year if we did that. By taking on more debt, we'll be in a totally different financial space in a much shorter amount of time."

"Very true. If we were to save up to buy each property in cash, we might as well just invest in the stock market and wait thirty years," Maya joked.

Jay laughed. "And we can't have that—we're old enough as it is!"

"Ha! Being old is a state of mind," teased Maya. "And this whole experience of investing in real estate is truly enlivening. I feel younger because of it, to be honest."

"You look younger than ever!" Jay teased. "But in all honesty, it's so much fun to be on the same page with you, working on our goals, and building our future together. Never did I think that real estate investing would bring us even closer as a couple. I am stoked for our future—so much so that I feel five years younger, too!"

Maya laughed. "As long as you just don't let stuff like graffiti give you gray hairs, huh?"

UNEXPECTED DWELLERS

The cash-out refi on the Atlanta duplex went smoothly. They used it to purchase the fourplex on Lincoln Street. About a month after closing, Maya's phone rang as she headed out of the hospital at the end of her shift.

It was Jay. "You will never guess what I just discovered," he said, not even saying hello.

"What's wrong?" Maya asked, feeling immediately alarmed.

"I went over to the Lincoln Street fourplex today to meet the contractor about the renovations we'll be doing and there were people *living* there."

"Wait, but the building is empty," said Maya. "So, we have... squatters?"

"Yes, exactly," said Jay exasperatedly.

Maya didn't even know what to say at first—this was not a situation she ever expected.

"I guess the contractor walked in and saw dirty, old patio furniture cushions laid out in a closet with some clothes and blankets. Stuff was written on the walls in marker. It was clear people were living there. When I got there, I walked around and found clothes in the dryer. They were doing laundry and everything."

The anger and stress in Jay's voice was obvious.

"Maya, what do we *do*? This is way out of my league, how do I even get squatters out?" Because Jay was self-managing the property, this was something he'd have to deal with directly.

"It'll be okay, Jay, I'm sure we can figure it out," Maya said, trying to be reassuring. It was clear Jay was freaking out.

"*Is* it okay, Maya?" Jay said, sounding very upset. "I mean, what are we doing? We're investing in these fixer-upper properties. And they're being taken over by squatters who are probably drug dealers and who knows what else! *I'm* supposed to be managing all of this. We are doctors, Maya! We take care of people, and now I have to figure out how to kick them out of this property? How are we mixed up in something like this?"

"Jay, I know this is super upsetting, but remember what we said when the graffiti happened to the Atlanta property?" Maya asked. "We dealt with it and moved on. It was annoying, but it wasn't the end of the world. This is a season, it isn't forever. This is one small blip in the grand scheme of this journey. We'll solve this and move forward, and we will get stronger because of it."

Jay took a deep breath, which calmed his nerves down a bit. Still, he faced a big problem—how was *he* going to get rid of these squatters?

"We have a community," Maya reminded him. "And we can involve our team members. We can ask them for help. We're not alone. Remember it's who, not how. We'll figure it out by asking others."

Jay listened and refocused on what he needed to do. The first step was to call their property manager in Atlanta for advice on what to do. She'd probably dealt with things like this before. Their relationship with her was great, so Jay felt okay asking for a little help with their Washington property. Abby told Jay to call the police to help check on the property and to remove the squatter's belongings. Jay's next call was to the contractor to resecure the property. As soon as Maya arrived home from work, he gave her an update.

"Well, the police are aware and said they'll drive by a couple extra times a day for now. I also let the neighbors know, so they'll help keep an eye out for us, too," Jay said. "The contractor is going to install new locks on the windows and doors, and we'll get security cameras installed as well. The construction crew will be there daily for the next few weeks, after all that is done anyway."

"That all sounds great," said Maya. "See? Things are already looking up. Zoom out into the future, and five years from now, we'll be laughing about the time we freaked out because we had squatters in one of our properties. You can't say we aren't building memories that we're going to be laughing about when we're 80!"

"Ha, I suppose," said an exhausted Jay, trying to see the humor in the situation.

"Just remember, even dealing with this, this property still gets us closer to our goals—our why," Maya said, kissing him on the cheek.

Jay felt better. Still, he couldn't help but think this real estate journey was such a roller coaster.

TAX TIME, BABY!

By the end of year one, they were generating more than $40,000 a year in cashflow from their rental properties. While it didn't sound like a lot, this represented a significant amount they could use toward purchasing additional properties each year.

By spring of their second year of investing, Jay and Maya

experienced their first tax season as real estate investors—in the form of a tax refund from year one. Jay having real estate professional status had paid off. They had created enough of a tax loss from real estate through bonus depreciation and rehabbing to shelter $295,000 of their income.

Here's how it worked.

- On paper, the Atlanta duplex made Jay and Maya $15,000 in cashflow for the year. Their renters also paid down $3,500 of the principal of their loan.
- Jay and Maya wrote off bonus depreciation on the property, which was roughly 25 percent of its value, giving them another $65,000 loss.
- While the rehab had cost them $60,000, Jay and Maya were able to write most of it off. Combined with some other write-offs, they ended up writing off $45,000 in losses on their taxes.
- To sum up their Atlanta property: +$15,000 (cashflow) – $65,000 (bonus depreciation) – $45,000 (extra losses) = –$95,000 off their taxes

On paper, it looked like Maya and Jay were negative $95,000 on the property, even though they received monthly cashflow from it.

After including the numbers from their Washington duplex and the fourplex on Lincoln Street, they were able to take another $200,000 in tax write-offs—so their total tax write-off was $295,000. Jay leveraged his real estate professional status so he was not required to pay income tax on the $75,000 of the wages he brought in as a doctor working part-time. They also sheltered the $40,000 a year in cashflowing rental income, and almost two-thirds of Maya's income.

After all was said and done, they got a check for $75,000 from the IRS.

"Time to go shopping for more properties," said Jay with a smile after he opened the envelope.

"Who knew taxes could be so much fun!" agreed Maya.

LEARN MORE

Want to learn more about how you can make monthly cashflow on your rental properties, but still show a loss on your taxes? Here's a blog article with more information: semiretiredmd.com/life-cashflowloss.

CHAPTER 10

STEPPING OUTSIDE THE STATUS QUO

"Thinking that a job makes you secure is lying to yourself."

—ROBERT KIYOSAKI

Despite dealing with the stresses of building a real estate portfolio, Maya felt refreshed, rejuvenated, and energetic. Her positive outlook started to emanate in other areas of her life—including at the hospital, where she was still working full-time as a hospitalist.

Even things like her committee meetings didn't feel like such a drag anymore. After finishing rounding in the morning, she grabbed her patient list with all its scrawled notes and checkboxes in the margin and hustled down the hall to get to her culture of care meeting on time.

Maya joined this committee when she first started as a hospitalist—it was required that all doctors join at least one committee—and for years, she dreaded going to the meetings.

She'd show up late (she was always running from patient to patient trying to complete discharges before noon, after all!), she rarely participated or brought forth any new ideas, and she really resented having to spend her precious time stuck in them.

But lately, she'd found herself feeling more motivated and solution oriented. She *did* have some ideas. And today, she was going to share them.

She walked into the conference room ready to share a couple ideas she had about how to improve patient care on the floors by engaging physicians and teams of nurses in reviewing safety protocols quarterly. After she was done, the group had a lively discussion. More importantly, they walked away with next steps to explore in order to help her vision become a reality. It was the most productive meeting the committee had had in a very long time, in Maya's opinion anyway.

As Maya packed up her things after the meeting, a colleague and the head of the committee, Dr. Colin Khan, approached her.

"Hey Maya!" Dr. Khan called out. "Great meeting today. I liked your ideas, and your optimism was refreshing! For the first time in a while, I think everyone left genuinely excited. So thank you for bringing them to us!"

"Wow, thanks, Colin," said Maya. "You know what? I *am* excited. I think we have a lot of good potential ways to improve safety on the floors. I look forward to seeing what comes of it."

She smiled and headed back to the hospitalist team room. She had a few more patients to round on and an admission waiting for her before heading home later that night. As she stood in the elevator on the way to the IMCU, she thought about Dr. Khan's comment.

At first his words had surprised her, but as she reflected, she realized: She *did* feel excited about the potential for change—and that was not the norm of how most doctors walked around the hospital. This feeling was new and different—and invigorating for her. With her focus now turned more toward her and Jay's investment portfolio, she didn't feel so stressed and burned out with her job. She was no longer interested in spending time being upset or angry about hospital politics, and instead focused on what she could control with patient care and in her own life. She had learned to pivot to solutions quickly, rather than lingering in suffering, from real estate investing and was now applying it to her job at the hospital, too.

And, even though she was still working full-time, she felt much less dependent on her career as a clinician—because she didn't need her job to survive. This had surprisingly breathed new life into her medical career. She had started to enjoy sitting and spending time with her patients again. She didn't run from room to room, putting efficiency first. She noticed the difference she was making with the little things she did. She was now a source of joy in the hospital instead of contributing to the anger and frustration around her. And she began feeling the desire to share her experiences with others.

That's when Maya realized that, with the craziness of work and building their portfolio, it'd been months since she chatted with Ben. She decided to invite him out to dinner at a local Pacific Northwest staple to catch up.

"Hey, Maya, so sorry I'm late," said Ben as he approached the table. He looked a little frazzled and worn. "It was a long day at the hospital—I've had a patient who's been bouncing in and out of the hospital with CHF exacerbations, and yet, continues to eat McDonald's. You know how it goes."

He took his jacket off to place on the back of his seat before he sat down and continued. "And then Jenna called when I was in the car. Toby's been going through a sleep regression and she's exhausted and stressed out, and mad at me because I'm never home. She says I don't spend enough time with him. It's true—he doesn't even greet me at the door when I do come home anymore. He just goes to Jenna for everything. I mean, I don't know what she expects me to do. I have to work this hard to support us."

He sighed and gave Maya a half-hearted smile.

"Anyway, that's me," he said, exasperated. "How are you? It's been too long."

Maya smiled sympathetically. "It has been too long. And I'm good. Really good, actually."

"Yeah, you seem...good," said Ben, eyeing her suspiciously. "What's going on with you?"

Maya went on to tell Ben all about her and Jay's journey into real estate investing—from their discovery of this path in

New Zealand, to the course and Facebook community, to Jay earning real estate professional status, to now owning three investment properties and counting.

When she finished, he just stared at her for a minute.

"Don't you and Jay think you're a little, I don't know, out of your league investing in real estate?" asked Ben. "I mean, you're doctors, not financiers. I don't know, it seems pretty risky if you ask me, even if you did take an online course or whatever."

"You know, it's been the best decision we could have made for ourselves," said Maya, confidently. She wasn't about to be swayed by Ben's concerns, even with the obstacles they'd faced recently with their properties.

"Jay and I decided something had to change in our lives last year. It had to. And it had to change right now. I didn't want to walk around feeling out of control of my life anymore. I didn't want to continue on the same path week on, week off for the next thirty years. I needed to live the life I wanted to live, and this is allowing me to do it right now.

"And it hasn't always been easy," she continued. She told Ben about the graffiti, which had happened again to the same property. Their property manager in Atlanta had just emailed asking for approval to spend another $250 to remove it. Maya also told Ben about the squatters at the fourplex and how distressing that had been for them, particularly Jay.

"Wow," said Ben. "How did you stick with it after that? Having squatters would have done me in."

"That's how Jay felt when he discovered them, for sure," Maya said. "He questioned getting involved in real estate investing and his ability to manage our properties—everything. But whenever something happens that could derail us from our journey, we refocus on our why."

"What's a why?" Ben asked.

"It's our vision for the future we want, our reason for investing in real estate," explained Maya. "When things get hard and we feel like giving up, our why gives us the power to push through and overcome obstacles."

Maya told Ben her and Jay's specific why—to cut back practicing medicine to part-time if they wanted; to gain financial freedom to travel and spend time together; and to build generational wealth and inspire their future kids.

"That certainly is ambitious," said Ben.

"It is," said Maya, "but this vision has changed not just our financial situation, but my own outlook. My whole life, really. Jay and I have this new goal, and we are working toward achieving it together. My life isn't consumed by the day-to-day hospitalist drama anymore. I actually like practicing medicine again. I just focus on the little things I can control with my patients and show up and care for them with presence. I take things one step at a time. It's very refreshing."

"Well that's great, Maya," Ben said. "I don't quite see the vision you have, and I don't share the love of medicine, as it is right now, anyway. But I'm happy for you."

Maya thought he sounded a little annoyed.

"I just hope it doesn't come crashing down on you, ya know?" he said with a sigh. "I'd hate to see you lose it all after all these years of working to be a doctor, resident, and now hospitalist."

He checked his phone.

"Argh, speaking of: that's the hospital. One of my patient's families wants a call. It's literally 6:58. And Jenna's sent me about ten texts," he said. "Listen, I better take this to go and get home. But hey, thanks for this." He motioned to the half-eaten dinner spread out in front of him. "It was great to catch up. And good luck to you and Jay. I'm sure it'll all be fine." He threw two twenty-dollar bills on the table and walked out with the phone to his ear.

Maya sat there for a moment. She knew Ben's reaction was normal and a common one from people who just didn't quite understand why medical professionals would become real estate investors. After all, she'd already faced that pushback from her colleague, Olivia, and her father.

Still, she felt sad for Ben—to see him working so hard, not seeing that he had other options. He was clearly grinding his gears and she could see the toll it was taking on him physically and emotionally. There was little she could do, however, except continue to reach out and share her experiences. Perhaps he would change his tune over time.

Until then, she'd continue to focus on her and Jay's goals. While the journey wasn't proving to be easy, it was already well worth it.

CHAPTER 11

CRISIS OF CONFIDENCE

"If you're not failing, you're not pushing your limits. And if you're not pushing your limits, you're not maximizing your potential."

—RAY DALIO

Maya was in the kitchen one evening making dinner on an off week from the hospital when Jay walked through the door, looking exhausted.

"Hey, love," Maya said. "I feel like I haven't seen you in forever. You're always at the Lincoln Street property these days. How are the renovations coming along?"

Jay ran his hand through his hair. He does that when he's stressed, Maya thought to herself. Something's wrong.

"Things could be better over there," Jay said. Maya could see the worry in his eyes.

"This contractor's team is working at a sloth's pace, and this morning, the inspection for the electrical upgrades failed," Jay explained. "He also said he and his team would have the new light fixtures installed two weeks ago and they're still not done. We're just losing money with this guy, Maya. I think we might need to let him go."

"But didn't we already pay him the full amount for the work already?" she asked anxiously.

"Yes, we did, which was a huge mistake," said Jay. "But now I don't know what to do! It's been two months since we started work—that's $8,000 in lost rent. We can't keep on like this. I really don't know what to do."

Maya's eyes widened; $8,000 lost.

"If we let the contractor go, though, then we'll have to find another contractor, which will take more time, and we already paid him!" Maya exclaimed.

They paced around the kitchen, both taking turns stirring the food cooking on the stove, mulling over their next step. What were they going to do? This was more than just a few hundred dollars to remove graffiti or install security cameras—this was thousands of dollars...and counting.

Dinner was ready, but neither of them had an appetite. The pit of anxiety in each of their stomachs had taken up all the space.

"How much money will we lose if we let the contractor go?" Maya asked, finally breaking the silence.

"We paid him $10,000 for the renovations," Jay said quietly. "He's probably halfway done."

Maya closed her eyes when she heard that number. Ouch. That, plus the lost rent would put them down $18,000.

"The contractor says his team is still probably two months away from being done based on the progress they've made so far," Jay continued. "That's another $8,000 in lost rent. That's if everything goes well. I don't trust this guy anymore."

"Me neither. I don't think we have a choice," Maya said. "We have to let him go. But how are we going to find someone new? Someone who can get the work done quickly?"

They jumped on their laptops and posted to the Facebook community. "Does anyone have a contractor north of the Seattle area who is familiar with rentals who they'd recommend?" Maya typed. Soon, referrals started coming in—and Maya and Jay jumped into taking action.

Jay called their agent to cross-reference some of the referrals to see if he knew any of them and could point them to the best one. After a bit of back and forth, they narrowed it down to two potential candidates to interview.

In the meantime, they called and fired the contractor. Jay and Maya tried to recoup some of the money for the work the contractor failed to do, but he refused, saying there was much more work than he had initially anticipated.

"Should we pursue small claims court?" Jay asked Maya.

"Maybe?" Maya answered. "I'm not sure it will be worth our time, to be honest. You have to think of the time and energy it would cost to pursue him. That's time and energy taken away from the more important things—like buying more properties."

"Agreed. Let's just find a new contractor and move on. I want to focus our energy on making this and future rentals work, not on pursuing the guy."

After doing their due diligence and cross-referencing some of the referrals, they invited two contractors to walk the fourplex and submit bids. Neither of them were cheap, but one stood out from the other.

"This one feels more thorough, and I like his detailed recommendations," Maya said, looking over the bids. "It's a bit more than I'd like, but time is money, and we need this work done... like yesterday."

"True," Jay said. "I'm okay with the price as long as we don't lose another month of rent. Oh and also, I'm not paying him up front. Let's pay him in chunks as the work is being completed. We won't pay him the final payment until after the work is completed and inspected. I finally got to watching those renovation modules on the membership site, and that's what they suggested doing, too," he said a bit sheepishly.

"That's a great idea," Maya said, relieved that they could put this behind them soon. She reached her arms out to give Jay a hug. He embraced her.

"Life either gives you what you want, or it gives you the lesson you need," Maya said.

"Ain't that the truth," Jay responded. "I definitely got the lesson I needed. Next time I'll set up the contract correctly and move much faster on firing if things aren't working out."

Throughout the rest of the rehab, Jay and Maya diligently checked in on the work as it progressed. The new contractor was awesome—the referrals were spot on—but if they'd learned anything, it was to *"trust but verify."*

Within a few weeks, the work on the property was completed. But when Maya and Jay sat down to review the financials for that property, panic once again set in.

"We're $30,000 in the hole on this property," Maya said gloomily. "That's our entire down payment."

Despite speedily finishing the renovation work, they still had to pay the second contractor to do the same work, which cost more money—and the units remained vacant longer than anticipated, meaning more lost in rent.

"I can't believe this is happening," Maya said, nearly in tears.

"Maybe your father was right," Jay said. "We're going to lose it all over a bad investment. We had no idea what we were doing hiring that first contractor, and now look what happened. We're in over our heads."

Maya's father's words haunted her.

Real estate is very risky, Maya.

You could find yourself broke, unable to pay your bills because you built up so much debt and bad investments.

You'll lose it all.

"Maybe we aren't good at real estate investing," Jay said. "Maybe we should give up while we're ahead..."

"Give up?" Maya said, cutting him off. "But what about our goals? Everything we're doing this for? What about our why?"

"Yes, Maya, but is this property getting us there? I don't think so!" They both were becoming increasingly upset. "I've cut back on medicine, but at what cost?" Jay continued. "We don't have time freedom—I'm constantly at that property overseeing things. You are still working full-time plus doing this, and I am working more than ever. And now, we're losing money! What are we even doing?!"

They both went quiet. It was the first time they'd argued over real estate, and it felt...awful. This wasn't the goal of this journey. At that moment, Maya, too, wondered if they were on the right path.

They decided to take a walk to cool off. For quite awhile, they walked in silence. But the fresh air had a calming effect for both of them, and it cleared their minds to think. Finally, Maya spoke: "If we aren't winning, we're learning," she calmly said with a slight whisper. "And right now, we're learning."

Jay stopped. "What?"

"We will learn from this and become stronger real estate investors because of it," Maya said. "We can't give up now, Jay. We've come so far. And this is our future. I know we are going to build the lives we want through investing in real estate—I just know it. This is just an expensive learning experience—that's all. The biggest lesson to come out of this, I think, is to always keep your eye on the bigger picture, and to not let the challenges along the way derail you from your ultimate goal. We'll use these lessons to minimize our mistakes in the future. But just like the graffiti and the squatters, this is a season. We'll solve the problem, learn from it, and move on."

There was a prolonged silence.

"Yeah...okay," Jay finally said. "Challenges, obstacles, setbacks—they're bound to happen. The one thing I know is we can get through anything. We are resourceful people. We are capable. Together, we will move forward."

They walked home hand-in-hand, both feeling tired, yet ready to move on. The peaks and valleys of real estate would continue. There would be high points and some low ones, but they were committed to becoming better investors, more resourceful individually, and stronger as a couple along the way.

CHAPTER 12

DREAMING BIGGER

"Do not follow where the path may lead. Go instead where there is no path and leave a trail."

—RALPH WALDO EMERSON

The renovation woes of the Lincoln Street property had renewed Jay and Maya's understanding that their real estate journey wouldn't be perfect, but that they could learn from mistakes to minimize them in the future. And with that realization came an unexpected side effect: confidence.

"You know, with every challenge we face, the more I'm starting to trust our decision-making and our teams," Jay said to Maya one night at dinner. "I'm starting to feel like we can handle anything."

"I agree," said Maya. "Even though we've had some ups and downs in our investment journey, every unexpected occurrence has given us the opportunity to take a step back and see a global view, instead of just riding the roller coaster of our emotions."

"Like we always say, 'We're going to look back at this when we're eighty years old and laugh,'" said Jay. That phrase had become one of their shared jokes as they navigated the waters of building their portfolio.

"So true," Maya said with a laugh. "I think we've grown to be more empowered with every challenge we face because we deal with it head-on and together as a team. Self-confidence truly does come from yourself, not from others."

"And from doing hard things," Jay added. "Every problem we face shows us what we're capable of."

They looked at each other and nodded. They had learned that lesson firsthand.

GOING BEYOND "REASONABLE"

As a secondary effect of the confidence they'd developed, Jay and Maya began to have an expanded sense of what was possible for them, too.

"I've noticed that when creating a goal or faced with a challenge, a lot of people focus their attention on what's 'reasonable' or 'based in reality,'" Maya said one night over homemade cheesecake. "They look at what everyone around them thinks is possible first. I feel like we're starting to look beyond that, though. Now we start with what we really want first. Then we look at how we can make it happen."

"I think you're right," Jay agreed. "I mean, we lived that way most of our lives, too. I think we are all trained by our culture and our parents and everyone to be 'reasonable' when we dream. It's part of a self-protective mechanism, you know? That way you are much less likely to, you know—quote, unquote—fail."

"Yeah, but aiming low from the beginning holds us back," Maya said. "When we never even consider that certain things might be possible for us, we don't even make an effort to get there. We limit ourselves by deciding to fail ahead of time."

"We've certainly had a lot of practice in pushing our—quote, unquote—boundaries, though recently, haven't we?" Jay said, making the quotation symbols with a smile.

"Ha, yes, that's certainly true," said Maya, nodding vigorously in agreement. "But we've accomplished so many things that didn't seem 'realistic' to others and even to ourselves when we first started, but ended up being totally possible. And each time we've overcome 'impossible' challenges, it's made me believe in us even more and our ability to do anything we put our minds to, even when others say it can't be done."

"I think that's made us just dream even bigger," Jay added. "I mean, think about some of the plans we've been making? They're *out there* even by our standards a few months ago!"

With the increase in confidence and belief in themselves, Jay and Maya were now considering purchasing properties that would require tackling larger rehab projects—properties that would need full kitchen remodels and buildings that would need to be gutted from top to bottom. They were talking six-figure rehabs. They had also started looking at larger prop-erties—ten- and twelve-unit apartment buildings—and had been considering tackling new markets in the United States and maybe even abroad.

"I really feel like nothing can stop us," Maya said. "For the first time in our lives, we really are living beyond 'reasonable.' We're living an *unreasonable* life. And the sky's the limit."

"And we'll just continue to reach higher and higher," added Jay.

HIGHER VALUE

As an offshoot of their investing experience, Jay and Maya had also learned to value themselves and their time—in real estate and outside of it.

"Hey, so good news!" said Jay one day as he walked in the door after a day of work. "My salary negotiation discussion with my supervisor—it worked! I got a 20 percent raise."

"Oh wow, Jay!" Maya said, hugging him. "You completely deserve it, love. You deliver so much value to that clinic in the way you care for your patients and pick up so many extra walk-ins each week." She squeezed him a little tighter. "I guess you've honed your negotiation skills now that we have a few property purchases under our belts, huh?" she joked.

"Ha! I have!" Jay laughed. "I approached it the same way we do after we get a bid from our contractor about what needs to be fixed. I told her my time is worth more than I'm currently being paid given all the additional value I bring to the clinic. Then I outlined what I should be paid and used actual data to back up my statements, and she agreed!"

"And now we'll have even more money to buy properties!" Maya nudged him playfully.

"Which reminds me, actually; what do you think about adding a short-term rental next?"

DIVERSIFYING THEIR PORTFOLIO

Maya and Jay now had three properties in their portfolio—a total of eight doors. Up until this point, they had only invested in long-term rentals. But with the cashflow coming in, Jay's raise, extra cash in their savings, cash from the cash-out refi, and the IRS check from the previous year, they had additional funds to buy another property immediately.

After a spirited debate, Maya and Jay decided the next step was to challenge themselves to learn something new. Buying a short-term rental (Airbnb/vacation rental) would allow them to diversify their portfolio and substantially increase their cashflow.

"Short-term rentals are generally higher risk," Jay said to Maya one night over dinner. "But, they have some benefits over long-term rentals."

"How are they higher risk?" asked Maya.

"Well, people often buy expensive single-family homes in vacation areas to use as short-term rentals. These types of properties can bring in a lot of cashflow, but they are riskier because a lot of money is tied up in one expensive property, and you are catering to only one type of renter: the vacation renter. So when there's a downturn and people reduce their vacation spending, it can affect your bottom line dramatically. Plus single-family homes tend to lose value when house values go down during a recession. That's not always the case with multifamily properties."

"They might be riskier, but short-term rentals have a higher potential cash-on-cash return, don't they?" said Maya. "We'd likely make a lot more per month because people are renting per night, so we can charge a much higher premium than if someone is living there. With what we already have in our portfolio, if we added a high-performing STR, we could get a third of the way to our goal."

That fact in itself made it worth considering an STR in both their minds.

"It would also provide an easier way to get tax savings, too," Jay continued as they mulled adding STRs to their portfolio. "If I decided not to go for real estate professional status this year, we could still use the phantom losses from depreciation of any rehab on our short-term rental to shelter our W-2 incomes."

He was referring to the short-term rental tax loophole they'd learned about during the course.

"Right," said Maya, agreeing. "That's if you meet one of the IRS's rules for material participation—for example, if we spend one hundred hours on the property and more than anyone else in the first calendar year—we can use the depreciation on that property to shelter active income. If we buy a big enough property, or maybe two STRs, we might even be able to shelter our income from taxes next year, even without you having real estate professional status. We could then use that cash to buy more properties and use bonus depreciation to shelter the income for future years, too."

"Is everything about getting more cash to buy more properties?" teased Jay.

"Of course it is!" Maya laughed.

"We could easily spend one hundred hours on the property in the first calendar year overseeing a small rehab, getting furniture, setting it up, and decorating it. Even if it is in another state. We'd just need to budget about a week to go there and set it up. We probably should also self-manage just to make sure we do more than anyone else," Jay added.

"Ooo, yes. That's a great plan," said Maya. "Get material participation, use bonus depreciation to generate a large paper/phantom loss, shelter our clinical income, and get a chunk of money back next year in saved taxes to keep growing. And then this year, you don't have to worry about qualifying for real estate professional status if you don't want to."

LEARN MORE

For more information about the tax benefits of STRs, visit semiretiredmd.com/life-strtax.

"That is true. But with all the work I'll be doing overseeing our portfolio of long-term rentals and the tax savings we get from that, I'm still planning on getting my hours in for REPs," Jay said. "There are some other considerations we need to discuss with a short-term rental, though. If we choose to invest in a single-family home instead of a multifamily property, its value tends to be tied more tightly to the market. So when a downturn comes, we have to be prepared to see our property drop in value."

He continued. "Another downside is that buyers looking for a home don't tend to buy single-family homes based on short-term rental income. They usually buy them based on how they appraise next to comparable properties in the area. In a downturn, the home likely wouldn't appraise at the value we'd want to sell it at if we decided to exit when prices are depressed. That's pretty different from what we find with long-term rentals where investors are willing to value a property and buy it based on past cashflow."

"It's not as easy to force appreciation predictably, either," added Maya. "You know how with long-term rentals, we can make huge leaps in wealth once we rehab a place and increase income? Well, increasing the net operating income of a short-term rental that's a single-family home doesn't necessarily mean we'll be able to charge that much more in a sales price when we turn around and sell it."

"But," Jay interjected, "if we force enough appreciation by making smart upgrades or changes that a primary home owner would value, we can still give ourselves a buffer if there is a downturn or we decide to sell the property. We could upgrade the kitchen design or bathrooms or even improve the outdoor space, for example. If that happens, there's a good chance we'll still walk away with a profit."

"A short-term rental is also riskier because there's only one roof," Maya said thoughtfully, adding to the list of considerations. "When it's vacant, it's completely vacant. And, don't forget that short-term rentals are more work because of the turnover of guests every few days."

They looked at each other. Those were quite a few downsides.

"But a short-term rental could really increase our cashflow," said Maya. "I remember one doctor in the community saying that her short-term rental had a cash-on-cash return of almost 40 percent!"

"Self-managing would also further increase our cashflow, since we wouldn't need a property manager," Jay added. "That would save us 25 percent in fees. And we could look at other STR options, too, like buying an STR in an urban center, so we cater to other customers besides just vacation renters. That would decrease some of the risks when a downturn comes. We could look for small, multifamily properties to see if they could be operated as STRs, while having the backup plan of making them long-term rentals. I see a lot of people doing that in the community. That would mitigate a lot of the risks."

Despite the downsides, Maya and Jay believed adding a short-term rental to their portfolio was a great avenue for accelerating their wealth. The real estate course they had taken talked a lot about creating balance across their portfolio. Since short-term rentals were higher risk, most people's portfolios in the community weren't filled with just STRs alone. They usually had long-term rentals, too. But adding a few STRs could be lucrative and help them grow their cashflow quicker.

Another perk: a vacation home they could use themselves!

"I think we should add two short-term rentals to our portfolio," said Jay, "and aim for twenty long-term doors by the end of the year. That's a ratio of 1:10, which would allow us to reap the benefits of both types. I'd feel comfortable with that for now. Down the road, though, I'll want to add more long-term rentals to further reduce our risk."

"That sounds good," said Maya. "Down the road, we could consider turning some of our long-term multifamily rentals into short-term or mid-term rentals, too. With mid-term rentals, we could target people like traveling nurses and others needing thirty to ninety-day stays—and we would get higher cash-on-cash return than we get with our long-term rentals for the same property. If there is a downturn, we can always turn those units back into long-term rentals."

It was a solid gameplan. They now had a strong foundation in long-term rentals and they felt confident branching out to different types of rental properties. If their short-term rental had an off month or two, they knew their long-term rental income could keep it afloat.

CHECK YOUR STR NUMBERS

Access our short-term rental cash-on-cash calculator here: semiretiredmd.com/life-strcoc.

ADDING AN STR

It didn't take long for Maya and Jay to find a short-term rental that looked promising. By September of their second year of investing, they'd found their place. It was in Gulf Shores, Alabama—a four-bedroom, two-bath listed for $730,000, located one street back from the beach. Nestled in a popular vacation spot, the house was already being used as a short-term rental and brought in about $95,000/year.

"The cash-on-cash return on this could be really, really good," Jay told Maya as they reviewed the bid from the contractor. "There's not much wrong with the bones of this place. Some new furniture, updated design features, maybe $15,000 to touch up the kitchen, and it'll have a totally upgraded feel. Based on what the property manager is telling us and what I've seen online in my searches, with those upgrades, the property will be competitive with higher-end properties, and we could get the rental income closer to $130,000/year."

The deal closed that month and Maya and Jay got straight to work managing the rehab from afar. Because the rehab was minor—mainly installing new counters and painting the cabinets and the interior—they kept the contractor hours lower than they'd spend self-managing the property, thus meeting the "one hundred hours or more than anyone else" rule for material participation.

The next month, they flew out to set it up and get it ready to rent.

"I'm so thankful for those recommendations we got from the course community for a contractor, handyman, and housekeeper for this place," said Maya on the flight to Alabama. "They'll be the help we need to allow us to self-manage."

Once they arrived, Maya and Jay ensured the updates and paint throughout the house looked as they should. They then got rid of some of the old furniture and started setting up the new furniture that had arrived, decorating the place, and building their listing on Airbnb and Vrbo. Once their property was ready, they lined up a photographer to get professional photos for the listing. In total, they spent around $25,000 to make the place feel like new, and had a lot of fun making design choices that would appeal to Gulf Shore vacationers.

By the time they flew home, they'd spent well over one hundred hours between the two of them on their property when adding together the time spent in due diligence purchasing it, the time overseeing the kitchen upgrade, the time spent pre-planning and ordering the furniture before their visit, and then the setup time while on site. That meant they met the IRS's material participation rules, so they could reap the incredible tax savings of sheltering part of their active incomes using bonus depreciation their first year owning the property via the STR tax loophole.

Here's what their tax savings calculations ended up looking like:

- $145,000 in bonus depreciation + $25,000 in furniture write-offs + $15,000 immediate expenses from the kitchen rehab and house repairs (much of this they were able to either expense or bonus depreciate) + write-offs for travel expenses, meals, miles driven, and the rental car

All in all, with the upgrades made, Jay and Maya increased rent to the point their short-term rental made them $130,000 a year—$80,000 of that being cashflow since they were acting as their own property managers. In that first year, they could claim almost $180,000 in a tax shelter since they met criteria for material participation. If they paid taxes at a 25 percent rate, they would save approximately $45,000 in income taxes just with this one property using bonus depreciation.

By the last week in October, the place was ready to rent. Maya and Jay were thrilled that their portfolio had grown in a balanced and diversified way, and they were getting even closer to their ultimate goal—financial freedom.

1031 EXCHANGE AND THE VELOCITY OF MONEY

By April of the following year, Maya and Jay encountered a common real estate investor problem: they had run out of money (they'd even spent their tax refund check on rehabs of their current properties). The slow process of saving for another down payment meant that they wouldn't get another property until much later in the year.

This wasn't an unusual problem. In fact, as they learned through their investor community, at some point, pretty much all real estate investors "run out of money" when they're building their portfolios. That's because it's somewhat addicting to buy good cashflowing deals. And, once you have built great relationships with your team and own a couple of properties, you continue to get access to more great deals—often at a much faster pace because your team knows how you operate and likes working with you. As you get access to more and more great deals, you want to buy them all and increase your cashflow even more. As such, most investors eventually end up running out of money.

While most new investors think that they need to stop buying and save for additional down payments—that they need $50,000 saved from their salary before they can buy another property—that's not necessarily true.

"I think we've hit a point where we need to get creative in coming up with more cash for down payments," said Maya one morning as she perused Redfin, sipping her homemade latte.

"Yeah, we're really scraping the barrel these days with our funds," said Jay. "And the great deals just keep coming. Just last week, Abby, our property manager in Atlanta, mentioned that one of her investors was looking to get rid of a killer cash-flowing duplex fast as part of a 1031 exchange and Sophie, our agent in Spokane, has an off-market ten-unit in the pipeline. We just don't have enough money to buy all these great deals. Do you have any ideas where we can free up some more cash?"

"Well...," Maya thought for a moment. "What about selling one of our properties? I know it's only been a couple of years, but that could free up some cash. Or maybe there's one we could cash-out refi?"

"I have been reading how that's how investors grow their money," Jay said. "Many of them reuse the same money over and over again. It's called increasing the 'velocity of money.'"

"Oh right, I've seen that term, too," said Maya. "Most people do it using the BRRRR strategy. That's buy, rehab, rent, refinance, repeat. For example, we buy a $100,000 property, turn it into a $250,000 property through a smart rehab that costs only a fraction of the forced appreciation we end up getting, pull out all our money to purchase another property using a cash-out refinance, and then buy the next property and do it again with the same money."

"So doing another cash-out refi would qualify as growing our portfolio by increasing the velocity of money," Jay added.

"Or maybe we should do a 1031 exchange?" said Maya. "Selling one of our properties and getting all of that money to work for us in a down payment of our next, bigger property would be more efficient. Maybe we should consider that."

"Hmm, that's a possibility," said Jay. "Remind me how that works again?"

"A 1031 exchange is when you sell a property and, instead of taking the profit and paying tax on it, you roll it into another property in a tax-deferred manner," explained Maya. "To do that, you have to use a 1031 exchange intermediary, who holds the proceeds from your sale and then transfers it into the next purchase without you, the investor, ever controlling the money."

"That's interesting," said Jay. "Man, you learn a lot from all that reading you do!"

Maya laughed. "The other thing I've read about 1031 exchanges is there are a lot of rules around them, so you want to make sure you follow them closely and have an excellent 1031 exchange company on your team."

"I'm sure the community has one," said Jay.

"As long as you follow the rules and buy a bigger property, the funds from your sale go directly into your next property's down payment and it's completely tax deferred—you don't have to pay taxes on this transaction," Maya continued. "Eventually down the road, you will have to pay taxes if you sell that final property instead of 1031 exchanging it, although you can avoid deferred taxes if you die and pass the final property onto your kids under certain circumstances."

"Which is definitely an end goal for us," Jay said. "But it seems like both are good options. I'm not sure which to choose—1031 or cash-out refi?"

"Maybe we should ask the community?" suggested Maya. "I'm sure there are others who have made this choice and can give advice based on their experiences."

So they posed their question to their online membership community.

"You have something called lazy equity in the properties you own and have rehabbed," wrote one respondent. "So if you bought a property for $100,000 and you rehabbed it for $50,000, and now it's worth $300,000, you have hundreds of thousands of dollars sitting in that property. You can pull that money out with a cash-out refi, but it won't be all of it. You're only going to get about 70 percent of it and the other 30 percent will stay in that property. So it's more efficient to sell that property and put 100 percent of that money into work on the next property. Mobilizing 100 percent of money can result in more cashflow on your next deal."

"But remember you have to pay the cost of selling!" another community member chimed in. "So in that way, selling and 1031-ing is less efficient. Something to keep in mind."

"It comes down to: Do you want to own the property for another five years? If there are reasons that you don't, then a 1031 exchange can be a good option," wrote yet another member.

The next response hit home for Maya and Jay: "One huge benefit of 1031 exchange is the legacy building element. You can keep exchanging properties over and over and defer your taxes over the years because you can depreciate each property you buy. When you die, your kids get your property at its value at that point, so they don't pay back taxes on the taxes you deferred during your lifetime!"

"We're going to do this for the rest of our lives so we can pass this to our kids tax free," said Jay. "That's part of our why. To create generational wealth for our kids. So why don't we see if there's a property we'd consider selling so we can most efficiently grow our portfolio?"

"Oh I have one in mind. Let's 1031 the Lincoln Street property." Maya said. They had continued to struggle with problems at the Lincoln Street fourplex. "Even after removing the squatters and firing the first contractor, we just aren't getting that far ahead with that property compared to the others."

"I like that idea. The maintenance costs there are higher compared to our other properties, too," Jay added, looking over his Excel spreadsheet. "And tenant turnover is also higher."

"Which means we're not getting the cash-on-cash we initially projected," Maya said. "We've added a lot of value to it though. So let's harvest some of that lazy equity."

"We should 1031 it, then," Jay said. "I don't see wanting it in our portfolio five years from now."

"Neither do I."

Since they had already taken the tax savings using bonus depreciation on that property, doing a 1031 exchange made the most sense. That way, they wouldn't have to pay depreciation recapture. Plus, there were plenty of properties that their agents had been sending their way that would fit better within their portfolio. They just needed the down payment to buy one.

LEARN MORE

Want to learn more about 1031 exchanges? Check out our blog post by visiting semiretiredmd.com/life-1031.

Doing a 1031 exchange, however, meant taking on even more debt by adding a bigger loan to the portfolio. This worried Jay just a bit.

"How much debt is *too much* debt, Maya?" Jay asked. "Is there ever a point where we'd just stop buying properties because we have so much debt?"

"Well," said Maya. "I looked at our equity percentage recently, and we're sitting right around 40 percent equity in our properties, because we've forced so much appreciation. I feel pretty comfortable with that, since all of our properties are cashflowing so much, too."

"We have forced *a lot* of appreciation," Jay said.

"And also, we're in the growth phase right now," Maya added, reassuring him further. "We need to accept that we'll be a bit more leveraged at this period in our lives. But as we get older, we'll focus on paying down our portfolio instead of growing it so aggressively and our equity will grow. When we get into more of a preservation stage, we'll focus on lowering our risk and not being so leveraged. Until then, let's just make sure every property cashflows well and have decent cash reserves just in case."

Jay felt better knowing they had a plan they felt confident in and funds set aside for rainy days. Growth was the aim right now. So they moved forward with building the portfolio that would take them into their future.

CHAPTER 13

FINANCIAL FREEDOM

"Most people overestimate what they can do in one year and underestimate what they can do in ten years."

—BILL GATES

Three years later.

"Maya, can you believe it's been five years since we started this real estate journey?" Jay said one night while he and Maya surfed Netflix documentaries to watch.

"I can and I can't," reflected Maya. "I mean, it feels like yesterday we started this adventure, but then when I think about how much our life has changed, it's pretty remarkable."

"It's completely reshaped the way we think about work and how we spend our time," Jay added.

"We actually do live life on our own terms just like we dreamed we would," said Maya. "It's pretty amazing!"

"I mean, how wild is it that we're financially free?" chimed in Jay. "I mean—I knew we could do it. But, it's something else to actually be here having done it! It's just such a wild feeling to know we did something that felt so big and scary at the time."

"And best of all, we've started our own little family," said Maya joyfully, glancing at the baby monitor sitting on the coffee table. "And you better believe she and her future siblings are going to grow up knowing how to make money from cash-flowing real estate, too."

THE NUMBERS

At this point, Jay and Maya's portfolio included twenty long-term rental doors and two short-term ones, bringing in $250,000 a year in real estate income—far exceeding their initial goal when they first started their investment journey.

Maya was a part-time hospitalist now, working one week per month. She worked because she wanted to—choosing to practice, rather than feeling forced to because she was dependent on the income. She had also helped codevelop a hospitalist fellowship training program, so she was spending more time teaching, which she loved. Her passion for her profession had been rejuvenated, and she loved interacting with her patients, teaching the fellows, and collaborating with her colleagues.

With their total annual income hovering at $400,000 (while still harvesting the tax savings of real estate, meaning they were paying minimal taxes), Jay had completely stepped away from corporate medicine, which, for him, was a refreshing change. He was now spending his time managing their real

estate portfolio, still meeting the criteria for real estate professional status (REPS) to shelter their cashflow and Maya's
income from taxes, and using his family medicine expertise to
volunteer. Several days per week, he traveled around the city
providing medical care to those in need and training residents
to do the same. He also provided financial education to young
doctors, seeing it as his way of helping to change the medical
system for the better. Finally, he and Maya had added in doing
one medical mission trip per year together.

KIDS, FAMILY, AND TRAVEL

At home, Maya and Jay were now parents to a one-year-old and
a three-year-old, and they used their newfound freedom to
enjoy their kids' childhoods. They went on family walks and
bike rides around the city, cooked amazing meals, and took life
in without being tied to a 60+-hour-a-week schedule.

Maya was able to switch her shifts around so they could travel
for as much as six weeks at a time, and they used those trips
to visit their aging parents, as well as take what they called
"adventure trips" with their kids. Most recently, the family had
traveled to Cappadocia, Turkey, where their three-year-old
daughter got a complete kick out of the "fairy chimneys" and
the family took a balloon ride overseeing the region.

For Jay and Maya, these were experiences they would never
forget, and they felt so fortunate—and free—to be able to do
them.

"So I booked the plane tickets to Portugal," Jay mentioned to
Maya one day as they were cooking dinner.

Their next six-week adventure was to Portugal, Greece, and Italy. They were taking their kids and also treating Maya's parents to a vacation.

"Oh great! My mom told me yesterday she's already started packing," Maya said with a laugh. "I'm grateful we can do this for them. It might be one of the last international trips they can take with Dad's dementia progressing."

"I emailed the agent over there to set up our appointment to see some short-term rentals in Porto, too," Jay said. During their visit, Maya and Jay hoped to find a short-term rental in Portugal, making it so they could even write off part of the trip as a business expense and have a future place to vacation as a family.

"Amazing, thank you," said Maya. "I traded my last two swing shifts with some of the other doctors at the hospital, so I'm all set to be off for those weeks."

Their real estate success had taken the pressure off her work at the hospital, and it showed. Maya was way more relaxed when she went in for her shifts, and she wasn't as drained after a busy week. She focused on showing up her best for her patients and could really tune out the bureaucracy and drama that distracted so many of her full-time (and burned-out) colleagues.

She chose to be there. She chose to see patients. She chose to practice medicine.

She was truly the happiest she had ever been.

TAKING ON THE SYSTEM

While Maya felt miles away from the feelings of burnout she'd experienced just a few years ago, when she looked around the hospital, she still saw it everywhere. There were *so many* unhappy doctors and staff members.

The hospital demands hadn't changed. Most hospitalists—including Ben—worked one week on/one week off at the hospital, from 7:00 a.m. to 7:00 p.m., and picked up several swing shifts per month from 4:00 p.m. to 12:00 a.m. It made for long days and weeks, and Maya could see the exhaustion on the faces of her colleagues. She felt guilty, at times, for the way she bounced around the hospital, stress free and happy while they trudged through the hallways with the weight of the world on their backs.

The requirements of being a modern doctor in a broken medical system had never sat well with Maya, but now that she had liberated her family's financial future from her medical career, she suddenly felt motivated and empowered to do something to try and change the situation for others.

If she saw things she didn't think were right, she spoke up.

She had become an advocate within the hospital for the hospitalist program, pointing out issues that needed to be addressed for both her colleagues and patients. She started attending more committee meetings because she felt passionately about improving the culture of medicine for the doctors. She became a force inside the hospital as a pioneer for change for the sustainability of all medical professionals.

She also tried to show her colleagues what was possible for them if they invested in cashflowing real estate. This came up naturally as colleagues questioned and admired Maya's change in demeanor—and lighter work schedule.

"I haven't seen you around in more than a month, Maya!" said one colleague while Maya was standing at the printer in the hospitalist team room waiting for her list to finish printing. "Where have you been?"

"We took our family to Turkey for six weeks, and I switched a few other shifts around, so yeah, I haven't been here for almost two months!" Maya replied.

"And I heard Jay isn't practicing anymore?" said another hospitalist. "How are you doing this?"

Questions like these were a natural entry point for Maya to explain exactly how she and Jay had built this life they led. In doing so, Maya tried to show her colleagues what was possible through building a portfolio of income-producing rentals and encouraged them to explore it for themselves.

She viewed it as another way she could give back to her fellow doctors, change the system for the better, and try to instill the dramatic shifts she knew were so desperately needed. She realized how much she—and her patients—benefited by her being financially free. She wasn't weighed down by just surviving.

Why couldn't all doctors live and work the same way? she reasoned.

Maya and Jay's real estate investing achievements had changed their lives, and they longed to facilitate that success for others. They aimed to use their wealth to do something big, not just for themselves and their family, and for other doctors, for that matter—it was for the betterment of the world.

REACHING THEIR GOALS

Maya walked in the front door after finishing her latest shift at the hospital.

"Hey, love," said Jay. "How was your shift?"

"It was really good," said Maya. "I think we finally made some headway on treatment for one of my patients who has been a frequent flier. I'd call it a win. I also sat in on the meeting about the new EMR billing and coding requirements, and I think they heard me when I said the doctors need scribes to help with the increasing charting demands, and that the hospital—not the doctors—should pay for them. Hopefully they take my feedback into account."

"Sounds like a successful day, then," Jay said and gave her a kiss.

It wasn't lost on either of them how much more at ease they both were—Maya was loving work, motherhood, and investing. Jay loved hanging with the kids, managing the properties, and had finally gotten back to his primary care roots with his volunteer work.

They sat back and reflected for a moment on just how far they'd come in the last five years. They'd gone from burned-out, stretched doctors who never saw each other to financially free investors who could take six-week-long trips with their amazing kids.

They were living a dream. It hadn't always been easy, either. It was the result of focus and persistence, driven by a strong why.

"But it's been worth it," said Maya, sinking in the couch.

"Yes, I would say it has," said Jay, putting his arm around Maya as they watched their kids play with their blocks on the floor in front of them.

CHAPTER 14

REUNION

"The future belongs to those who believe in the beauty of their dreams."

—ELEANOR ROOSEVELT

"Well hey there, long time no see," said Ben, walking up to Maya in the hospital. They had a rare swing shift together, and the hospital had been surprisingly slow all day.

"Hey!" said Maya. "Yes, it's been awhile! I haven't been working as much lately." She looked around. "Maybe I'm turning into a white cloud. How are you, Ben?"

"I'm alright," said Ben. "Yeah, it's been pretty nice here today." He paused. "Hey, since we have some time, do you want to go grab a coffee and catch up? I feel like it's been forever since we talked. Last time we got together, I was a little distracted. I'm sorry again about that." He smiled, almost embarrassed.

"Yeah, that'd be great." They headed to the hospital Starbucks and found an open table.

"Can you believe it's been six years this month since we got out of residency?" Ben asked.

Maya nodded and smiled. "Who would have thought we'd still be working at the same place, eh?"

"Yeah, but you're half-time now! And when I see you here, you're always bopping around all happy. How do you do that, work part-time? And with Jay volunteering? How do you make that work?" Ben said with a quizzical look on his face.

Maya explained just how, exactly, they were doing it. She shared how she and Jay envisioned a different future for themselves, one in which they didn't depend on their incomes as doctors to survive. She told Ben about their cashflowing properties and portfolio building, and how Jay claimed real estate professional on their taxes and continued to shelter her income from income taxes.

"The plan had been for us both to retire from medicine," said Maya. "But once we started this new life, it changed my perspective. My love for medicine came back. I didn't want to leave it completely. And now I feel like I have breathing room to have another purpose too: helping change the medical system for the better."

She told Ben all about the travel they had been doing with their kids. She talked about how she was spending more time with Jay than ever before, and how she cherished the time she was able to spend with her parents, who were getting older. Finally, she shared how she and Jay had been training residents in financial literacy.

"I'm utterly amazed," said Ben. "That's...inspiring, your journey. Makes me think it's time to start owning rental properties, too."

Ben went on to fill Maya in on his life.

"I mean, I can't complain—I have a beautiful wife, two great kids, a great house. Still have my Porsche!" he said with a laugh. "Although I haven't quite been able to upgrade it yet. But there's one big difference between my life and yours. I am dependent on my income as a doctor. I feel the stress that comes with that."

It was draining him, he admitted. Working week on, week off on top of all his other responsibilities as a doctor, dad, and husband—he felt like he was running all the time and never had a chance to breathe. He'd love to get back to why he went into medicine in the first place, to get to focus on the patients. But also take care of himself and his family at the same time, just like Maya did.

"I've been listening to you all these years, and I admit, I thought you were crazy," said Ben shaking his head with a chuckle. "But then I finally read *Rich Dad Poor Dad*, like you suggested last month, and I realized something: I *do* have to do something different. I don't want to be only an employee my whole life."

"I'm glad we can talk about this, Ben," said Maya. "One thing I learned on this journey is that people are ready at different times. It sounds like you might be ready to make a change."

"Maybe I am, but boy do I wish I started earlier," muttered Ben.

"Hey now, don't beat yourself up," Maya said. "You're exactly where you should be. No need to regret the past and dwell on things you should have done. It'll just drain your energy and slow you down. Just move forward and start taking action to make your future what you want it to be."

"I still have a lot of questions though," Ben said. "Like, I don't have a huge stockpile of savings to invest. The kids' private school tuition and the mortgage on the lake house eat up a huge chunk of my cash each month. Jenna's cut back her hours at work quite a bit, too."

Maya nodded. That was okay. "We didn't have a lot of money when we started five years ago either," she said. "We had our down payment for a primary residence we didn't end up buying—$150,000—and look what we've done. We've been able to force appreciation on each property by rehabbing, increasing rents, and tapping hidden value and then pulling money out of them to reuse and buy our next properties. We were focused and committed. That's how we grew our portfolio with so little to start. You can do that, too."

"Forcing appreciation, tapping hidden value, I don't even know what that means," Ben said. "I know *nothing* about real estate."

"Neither did we," Maya said. "I can help you. And the course we took, you can take that, too. And you can join the community of other doctors investing in real estate. We're still active in that group daily. It's full of people just like us, Ben. Doctors and other high-income professionals looking for something different. Something *more*. And as doctors, we understand each other. And we help each other, too."

"I still need to work full-time for the foreseeable future, so I won't have a lot of time to dedicate," Ben muttered.

"I continued to work full-time as a doctor while doing this the first few years, too. Yes, Jay cut back to claim real estate professional, but you wouldn't have to do that if you didn't want to. Or maybe Jenna could take the lead with the real estate journey!"

Ben's eyebrows shot up. *That could be a good idea*, he thought. But she may not be too eager to become a real estate investor.

"Not everyone's spouses or significant others want to learn how to invest in real estate," said Maya, reading Ben's mind. "And that's okay. There are plenty of people doing this alone. I'm telling you, Ben, embarking on this journey made full-time medical work fulfilling again. I had a bigger goal to go after and suddenly, the burnout from practicing medicine decreased. I mean, look at me! I love medicine again!"

Maya could see in Ben's eyes how he was thinking, questioning.

"Look, I get how you're feeling," she said. "All these walls you're seeing are called limiting beliefs. Limiting beliefs are the stories we make up about our own abilities or the way that the world works that hold us back from reaching our full potential. They are beliefs driven by fear. Overcoming these limiting beliefs isn't about getting rid of the fear. Fear is a natural part of the process. It's about having the courage to push through it and see you are capable of more, if you want it. And once you do, you gain confidence. It's a process, but you can absolutely do it."

"Wow, now you sound like an inspirational speaker," joked Ben.

"I'm saying all of this because I experienced the same things. Once you get started, you'll see it's possible for you too."

Ben smiled. He was starting to believe what she was saying and saw himself being able to successfully invest in real estate. Then his face turned serious.

"If I do this, what if I lose it all?" he asked.

She smiled reassuringly at him. "I was scared about that too when I first started out. Back when I didn't have the knowledge, the skills, or my team, things felt overwhelming. But then I realized I wasn't alone because the community had my back. Plus, there are ways to mitigate risk so that you don't lose it all. When you know what you're doing, it's much less risky. When you have a community to help you spot your blind spots, it's less risky. When you get used to looking at the downsides and planning for them if they do happen, it's less risky. And you know what, Ben? You can learn all those things. You're smart, and you're more than capable."

Ben nodded in agreement. "As doctors, we are used to learning skills and putting them to immediate work," he said. "We're used to relying on ourselves to figure it out. We're resourceful."

"That's right," Maya said. "You know...relying on just your clinical income is risky, too. What if something were to happen to you or make it so you couldn't practice medicine anymore? Having multiple sources of income is much safer."

"Oh," Ben paused. "You're right. I hadn't thought about it like that before."

"Look at the alternative if you *don't* do this," Maya went on. "You're going to continue living like you have been for another, what, twenty-five, thirty years? Do you want to do that? *Can* you do that? Is that really sustainable?"

Ben thought for a moment.

He hadn't been ready in the past because the pain of doing what he was doing wasn't strong enough—the burnout, the exhaustion, the feeling trapped and dependent on his income to survive. But now, the pain was front and center in his life every day, and it was getting increasingly unbearable. He could now see there was another way—a way others in the same position as him were following successfully. He had options. He had choices. He wasn't trapped at all.

"No," he said, coming to a decision in his head. "This current path is not sustainable." He took a deep breath and let it out slowly. "I'm ready to build a life I love. I'm ready to live life on my terms. I want to do this."

"Okay," said Maya, excited for her friend to have come to this conclusion.

"I'll help you get started."

CONCLUSION

Doctors are incredible.

When Kenji and I talked through how we wanted to end this book—how we should wrap up the story we just told—that was the first thought that came to our minds.

Because it's true—doctors are incredible human beings. You are already amazing. You have accomplished so much to get where you are today. You carry so many on your back: your patients, your staff, your family, your work, and your personal life.

And, on top of all of this, you also have the additional possibility and potential to learn how to build wealth through real estate.

We know this because we, too, were working more than full-time as hospitalists when we chose to take this journey together to build a real estate portfolio and claim financial freedom. Since we started Semi-Retired MD, we've also had the true joy and honor of watching many other doctors and high-income professionals and their families achieve financial freedom using real estate investments.

Financial freedom and living life on your terms is closer to you than you think. With diligence and focus, you are fully capable of reaching it over the next few years.

Consider how your personality and your training have prepared you to invest in real estate.

To start, you are driven—you were taught to go after your goals, and you make them happen. You're a hard worker. You are used to juggling many different balls at once. You bring your best to every situation and are extremely meticulous, ensuring you miss nothing, because if you do, it could mean life or death for your patients.

You spend every day trying to make things better. This makes you a great thinker. As a doctor, you were trained to look at innumerable pieces of data, pull out patterns, and then try to help. You were trained to look at worst-case scenarios and to actively think through situations and come up with the best solution. You were trained to mitigate risks.

You're also an active learner. Think of how you learned in medical school and residency—see one, do one, teach one! You learn it, you do it, and then you go teach someone else to do the same thing.

Add to all of this the fact that you have a solid job that's fairly downturn resistant, meaning you have the ability to secure residential loans. You're an optimal candidate for this journey.

Everything you've worked for, all those skills you've gained, they're all extremely transferable to real estate investing. Since you are driven and focused, work hard, mitigate risk, and set goals, what you can achieve is unlimited.

All you have to do is decide to start. Stop playing not to lose. It's time to play to win. It's time to decide to build a life on your terms.

IT STARTS BY INVESTING IN YOURSELF

"Whether you think you can or you think you can't, you're right."

—HENRY FORD

This quote is one that we come back to time and time again because it's just so true. Our own journey proves it.

It's the power of the mind. If you believe you can do it, you can do it. If you believe you can't do something, then you're also right. You'll never do it.

This is the opportunity to believe in yourself. As a doctor, you spend your days focused outward, helping others. Now is the time to turn that focus inward, to take care of yourself and your family, too.

Invest in you. Invest in your education, in your growing mind. It's the most powerful thing you have, and when you invest in it and believe in it, you can do amazing things.

You already did it once. You invested in yourself and your mind when you went to medical school. It probably left you hundreds of thousands of dollars in debt. That may make you angry, frustrated, or even sad. But the fact is, that's money you spent to invest in your mind, and the return is a lifetime of medical income. That has set you and your family up for decades of earning well above what most others earn in the United States.

This is your chance to do that again. Only this time, invest in your financial education to grow your and your family's wealth, achieve financial freedom to live your life on your terms, and secure generational wealth for your kids and your grandkids.

It all starts with believing and investing in yourself.

Make no mistake, this journey is going to take effort and energy. It will require determination to reach your goals. You will need to focus on your real estate business. Just as you saw in Maya and Jay's hypothetical journey, there will be challenges you will need to overcome.

But the payoff, achieving time freedom—and doing what you want, when you want, with whom you want—is everything. You only have one life to live, and we believe you deserve that freedom.

As was our experience—and that of Maya and Jay and many of our students—the real estate investment journey has the potential to reignite your passions for continual learning, collaboration with colleagues, your relationship with your significant other as you work toward your common shared goal, and even your practice of medicine.

Truly, real estate investing can be transformational. It changed our lives, and it has the potential to do the same for you if you decide to take the journey.

When you are ready, the resources to get started are here for you.

Start by exploring the free content available at www. semiretiredmd.com. Read our blog posts, which offer education on specific real estate topics in a clear, actionable way. We also share experiences from our own journey, including our personal experiences investing in real estate and the things we do to continue to grow our minds, wealth, and portfolio.

Subscribe and listen to our podcast, Doctors Building Wealth, where we talk with fellow doctors, financial experts, and members of our course community about their journeys and other entrepreneurial topics.

Join our Facebook group, Semi-Retired Physicians, to be part of a community of doctors and their significant others to talk about real estate. You can join that group by visiting semiretiredmd.com/life-fbphys. If you're a high-income professional, we also have a group for Semi-Retired Professionals. You can join that group by visiting semiretiredmd.com/life-fbprof.

Then, when you're ready to begin your own journey, consider joining us in our flagship course, *Zero to Freedom*, or our short-term rental–focused course, *Accelerating Wealth*.

Zero to Freedom guides you through the entire process of selecting and purchasing investment properties. Just like you saw with Maya and Jay's journey, the course is so much more than seven weeks of learning—it's an ongoing community to join and engage in as you expand your portfolio and grow your business. Meanwhile, *Accelerating Wealth* gives you the skills, knowledge, and team to profitably buy and run a short-term rental business.

COURSE WAITLISTS

To get on the waitlist for our flagship course, *Zero to Freedom*, visit semiretiredmd.com/life-ztf.

To get on the waitlist for our short-term rental course, visit semiretiredmd.com/life-aw.

Since 2018, Kenji and I have had the true privilege to watch many of our colleagues and high-income professionals achieve financial freedom through real estate investments. We've seen them take sabbaticals, switch to jobs that gave them more time with their families, cut back, start living half-time in Europe, become entrepreneurs and start other businesses, negotiate higher salaries, fall in love with medicine again, overcome burnout, pursue their hobbies, start training others in finances, and even win awards for being excellent physicians because they know their worth and now have the opportunity to work from a place of wholeness—not because they need their job, but rather because working as a doctor *had become a choice*. Many have chosen to continue to work as doctors, and those who do are fundamentally changed. Many of them are motivated to continue to grow themselves and to change the culture of medicine from the inside out.

Reducing our reliance on our medical incomes is how we change the culture of medicine for the better. When doctors practice and treat patients on our own terms—full-time or part-time, and because we want to be there, not because we're tied to our salary—that is when the stress washes away and our passion for medicine reignites.

That is how patient care improves.

As Kenji and I look forward to the future, we see our community of doctors and high-income professionals continuing to grow and spread the message to others who are toiling long hours, overworked, and missing time with their families—that it doesn't have to be this way.

You have spent years of your life dedicated to serving others. Now, dedicate time to yourself, your family, and your future.

When you do, you can practice medicine how you want and *live life on your terms.*

ACKNOWLEDGMENTS

This book is dedicated to all the doctors out there serving their patients. We know that you are driven to deliver the best care possible. We know that you care deeply about your patients. We know that you are working incredibly hard to balance the expectations of administrators, your patients, and your families. We know you have only a little left for yourself. The way you show up inspires everything we do at Semi-Retired MD. Our goal is to help 500,000 doctors and their families use real estate to achieve financial freedom and build lives they love. It is an honor to get to serve you by doing that every day.

This book is also dedicated to those who dare to dream. We know it's easier to continue to walk the path laid out by many before you. It takes courage to decide and aim for more. We have seen many of you take that leap into the unknown and come out transformed and victorious. We've watched you go through challenging times with grace. You've proven to yourselves what you are capable of doing by taking that first step of investing in real estate. We love seeing how that one door opens many more opportunities for you as you gain financial independence. It is a gift to watch you start to make your dreams a reality.

We'd also like to share a few thank yous.

We wish to thank the staff of Semi-Retired MD for their support along this journey. Our SRMD team members embody four core values: to have a growth mindset, take ownership, be solution-oriented, and to be of service to others first. Our team members are passionate about helping doctors and high-income professionals and furthering our company mission. They are devoted to doing the best work they can, always asking our company's guiding question: How can we make our students more successful? If it were not for them and the support they have given Kenji and me as we built this company and wrote this book, we would not have been able to help guide the number of transformations that we have across our community.

Finally, a very special thank you to our family. Kenji and I are lucky to have supportive parents who believe in us and what we are doing. They've helped free us up many, many times so we could deliver to our community. Our kids, likewise, have been patient with us as we travel extensively and strive to find the right balance between all our roles and responsibilities. They are one of the great joys of our lives and spur us to continued growth so we can pass down our skills and knowledge to them, our future real estate investors. We are truly blessed.

ABOUT THE AUTHORS

Leti is a board certified family medicine physician. She completed her undergraduate degree at Hamilton College and completed a graduate degree in development anthropology at George Washington University. After finishing medical school at the University of Vermont, Leti went to residency at Swedish Family Medicine Residency, followed by a hospitalist fellowship. She worked as a hospitalist from 2011–2020, working at Good Samaritan Hospital, Queen's Medical Center, and Swedish Medical Center before she transitioned to be nonclinical. She also started a healthcare documentation company with Kenji and served as Chief Medical Officer from 2015–2016. She currently splits time between running Semi-Retired MD, real estate investing, traveling, and raising their children.

Kenji is a board certified internal medicine physician. He completed his undergraduate degree at the University of Pennsylvania and medical school at Johns Hopkins. After medical school, his career path veered off the traditional path as he (in order): started a nutraceutical company, completed an internship at the University of Washington (UW) in

Seattle, worked as a management consultant for McKinsey & Company, returned to UW to repeat his internship (yes, two internships), and completed a full residency. After residency, he worked as a hospitalist at Swedish Medical Center in Seattle where he worked from 2008–2020 (minus the one year Leti and Kenji lived in Hawaii, where he worked as a moonlighter at Queens Medical Center). During his time at Swedish, he started two companies and successfully exited both of them. He currently works on various passion projects, including real estate investing, becoming a home sushi chef, hiking, and raising their children.

Together, Leti and Kenji started investing in real estate in 2015 after reading Robert Kiyosaki's *Rich Dad Poor Dad* on their life-changing vacation to New Zealand. Over the course of three years, they built up a sizable portfolio of cashflowing rental properties and learned to harvest the tax benefits of real estate to achieve financial freedom. As of this book's publishing, they own more than 150 cashflowing long- and short-term rental properties spanning over three states.

Leti and Kenji started Semi-Retired MD in 2018 to help educate and inspire other doctors to invest in real estate to build an alternative source of income that would allow them to work in medicine on their terms. To date, they have trained over 3,000 doctors and high-income professionals through their courses, *Zero to Freedom* and *Accelerating Wealth*.

When they're not educating other doctors and high-income professionals to achieve financial freedom, they can be found traveling all over the world with their children. They currently live in Puerto Rico.

Made in the USA
Middletown, DE
30 November 2023

44129353R00159